BEVERLEY

A Portrait of a Town at the Millennium

Text by
John Markham

Photographs by
Patricia E. Deans
and a team of colleagues

The members of the Beverley Millennium Publication Group, who compiled this book, were: Patricia E. Deans, John Goode, F. William Gray, Kate Gray and John Markham.

Photographs were taken by Patricia E. Deans, assisted by:

Members of Beverley Photographic Society: Tim Carter, Arthur Coates, Fay Day, F. William Gray, Kate Gray, Denis Gregory and Pete Smith.

Members of Beverley F.4 Photographic Society: Keith Beverley and Dave Robson.

and by Brian Dalton, John Goode and Tony Pinder.

Grateful acknowledgement is made to the following who have kindly consented to the reproduction of copyright photographs: Beverley-Lemgo Association, East Riding of Yorkshire Council, Hull Daily Mail, Rotary Club of Beverley, Sonar Research and Development Ltd. and David Walker of Huddersfield

The Beverley Millennium Publication Group wishes to express its thanks to all those who have assisted this publication by generous donations or help in kind: BA Print, Beverley and District Civic Society, Mrs. Mary Brown, Mrs. P. Byass, Mrs. Kate Goddard, Hull Historical Association, Mrs. B. Oughtred, and many others who have asked to remain anonymous, and all the many people, organisations and businesses which have been extremely cooperative and agreed to photographs being taken for this book, in particular for special permission given by all the church authorities, the Humberside Police and Humberside and South Yorks Army Cadet Force.

Front cover: *View from North Bar Within.*

Back cover: *Aerial view of Beverley (by kind permission of David Walker)*
                  Sun dial on the Minster.

Title page: *The Market Cross, Saturday Market.*
                 The White Horse (Nellie's), Hengate

Saturday Market.

British Library Cataloguing in Publication Data.

A catalogue record for this book is available from the British Library.

© 1999 Beverley Millennium Publication Group

ISBN 1 902645 07 3

Published for Beverley Millennium Publication Group by

Highgate of Beverley

Highgate Publications (Beverley) Limited
4 Newbegin, Lairgate, Beverley, HU17 8EG. Telephone (01482) 886017

Produced by

4 Newbegin, Lairgate, Beverley, HU17 8EG. Telephone (01482) 886017

Printed on 135gm Mediaprint Silk supplied by
G. F. Smith · London · Ltd., Lockwood Street, Hull, HU2 0HL

Foreword

by
the Reverend David Hoskin

One of my memories of school is of constantly being berated by the maths master for forgetting the units. 'Twenty-seven what?' he would ask. 'Elephants? Woodlice?' The answer in those distant pre-metric days was inevitably, 'Inches, sir' - or 'Pounds weight', or 'Feet per second'. He was a good teacher, for ever since I've been suspicious of mere numbers.

'2000 what?' I find myself asking, and the answer comes back loud and clear, '2000 years since the birth of Christ' (give or take a few inaccuracies in the calendar!). All are invited to the party, but, make no mistake, this is a Christian Millennium and to pretend otherwise is to rob the number of its significance.

Not that I have met many in this town who would want to separate the Millennium from its roots. Beverley owes much of its importance and architectural finery to the Christian faith. Medieval pilgrims to the shrine of St John of Beverley not only enabled the building of the Minster, but, through the consequent prosperity of local merchants, that of St Mary's Church also.

Glorious though its medieval buildings are, Beverley is not a town that has stood still. As this *Portrait* shows, building has continued down the centuries with particularly fine examples from the Georgian period, and some modern work of note also. It is not surprising that the Arts are strong here, with, for example, several choirs and three annual music festivals.

If the cultural life of the town continues to flourish, then so too does the Christian faith. Beverley has many thriving churches, both old and new. We are, as a community, well placed to celebrate in style the first 2000 years of the Christian era, and to enter the next Millennium with confidence.

Vicar of St Mary's Church and Rural Dean of Beverley on behalf of the Churches of Beverley.

Contents

Colour Illustrations

Pages 1, 2, 13, 14, 27, 28, 41, 42, 63, 64, 77, 78, 91, 92, 103, 104.

Introduction

by

John Markham

A good picture is worth a thousand words and nothing conveys the atmosphere of the past so powerfully as an old photograph. It is, though, the incidental details, the clothes, the cars and the goods in shop windows which often arouse more interest than the procession or great occasion which was the reason for the photographer putting his head under a black cloth and focusing his lens.

It was this thought which decided members of the Beverley Millennium Publication Group to produce a book which showed the town and the people as they were at the end of the 20th century, rather than another historical work on subjects which have already been well covered. What makes the early 19th-century histories of particular interest is not so much their – sometimes inaccurate – theorising about the origin of the town but the information they give about the institutions and events which were contemporary or within living memory.

No one knows which everyday objects and scenes will fascinate people of the future – and we are certain to have made mistakes – but we believe that our selection of pictures gives a not unfair impression of life in Beverley on the eve of the new Millennium.

Our great regret is that, however many photographs we included, many equally interesting ones have had to be left out. To those individuals, businesses and organisations which do not feature in this book we must stress that their omission is in no way an indication that they are considered less important than those which appear. The pictures which appear are merely a cross-section of the large number of excellent photographs taken by Patricia Deans and her team.

This is a book in which pictures are more important than words, but even a casual survey of these illustrations produces some inescapable conclusions. The loss of Beverley's staple industries has resulted in a fundamental change in its economy: new industries and the growth of tourism are helping to compensate for what has been lost, but only in the next century will the eventual outcome be known.

It is obvious, too, that shops and shopping have been subject to a social revolution over the last 30 years. Beverley was always a town of small family businesses where the relationship between owners and customers made shopping a friendly as well as a commercial activity. Though some such firms survive, supermarkets and self-service have had profound consequences for the pattern of trade, and older Beverlonians complain that – supermarkets apart – there is no longer a single grocer in the town centre. High rents and rates have caused serious problems for small businesses and anyone who strolls through the town is aware of empty premises and of new shops which last only a short time. A comment printed in a local newspaper ten years ago is still true: 'National stores are moving in, smaller firms find themselves squeezed out and there is speculation as to who will move into the many deserted properties.' The prevalence of rate-free charity shops is a controversial issue, and there are those who are unhappy to see so many building societies, banks and estate agents occupying key positions in the centre.

Traffic problems have become the bane of Beverley which everyone recognises but no one quite knows how to solve. One of the town's assets, free parking, has now been lost, but the Government's attempts to persuade drivers to abandon their cars and use public transport is unlikely to counteract the convenience of private motoring. Even the cattle which amble nonchalantly across the Westwood roads have experienced – often too literally – the impact of modern traffic. Pedestrianisation of central streets has enabled shoppers to use Toll Gavel and Butcher Row without too much risk to life and limb, but shops need regular deliveries, and transport cannot be wholly excluded from a town where people make their living through trade and industry.

Massive housing expansion into outer suburbs has met opposition from those who would like Beverley to remain the small town of their childhood, which grows ever more delightful as the distance of time lends enchantment to the view. The developments of recent years cannot be erased, though they can be modified, and one hopeful sign is the building of modern houses in the town centre and the realisation that urban dwelling has its advantages. A town without a heart is dead.

Some of the pictures in the pages which follow show that uncertainty about the future and the impersonality of modern life have a tendency to make people turn nostalgically back to a perfect age which never quite existed. Festivals and processions bring welcome colour and variety, and Beverley has plenty of knowledgeable and vigilant residents who react quickly and effectively to threats to the townscape, ensuring that no planning applications escape their all-seeing eyes.

Although nostalgia has its appeal, and conservation will always be important in a town with so many fine buildings, Beverley is not (like some well-known places) artificially preserved in aspic for tourists to visit and photograph. It is an historic town but it is also one where people live and work and which still has a reason for its existence. Long may it so remain.

View from the roof of the Minster looking south.

SUBSCRIBERS

Beverley Arms Hotel
Phil Stebbens t/a Beverley Camera
    Centre
Beverley Decorative and Fine Arts
    Society
Beverley Grammar School
Beverley Minster C.E. Primary School
Beverley St. Nicholas Primary School
St. John of Beverley R.C. Primary
    School
Carol Bird Interiors
Carmichaels of Beverley Jewellers
East Riding of Yorkshire Libraries
Robert Gail
John and Christopher Hillman,
    Master Butchers
The Hutton Press Ltd.,
Derek and Pam Hemingway
    (Moores Dairies)
Local History Unit, Hull College
Kingston upon Hull Libraries
The Nelson Webster Partnership
Simsons Photographers
Society of Friends (Quakers)

A
Gordon Abbott
John Bryan Acey
Gwyn and George Adams
Dr. Rosemary Adams
Tamasin Adams
Michabla Adams
Margaret Adamson
Stuart Adlington
Joyce and Gordon Ainslie
W. D. Aitken
R. J. Akrill
T. B. Akrill
    J. B. Smith (née Akrill)
    P. M. Hardcastle (née Akrill)
Peter and Valerie Allinson
Anthony Allsop
Mrs. J. S. P. Anderson
Betty Andrew
Norman Angell
Richard and Sandy Appleyard
Mark Ashbridge
James Mark Ashman
Harry and Eveline Aspden
Gareth and Cheryl Aspinall
Tony and Marion Atkin

Jean Atkinson
June Atkinson
Gordon Atkinson
Mary E. Atkinson
Peter H. Atkinson
P. B. Atkinson
Mr. N. M. Auton

B
Doris Herdsman Badham
Mrs. P. S. Baglee
John Bagshaw
Mrs. A. Bailey
Kathryn Bailey
Michael Robert Bailey
Rev. Canon and Mrs. David Bailey
Helen Baker
Michael Peter Baker
Stephen John Baker
Mr. and Mrs. T. Ball
Thomas Bangs
Tom Bardsley C.P.F.A.
David J. Barker
Roy and Barbara Barker
Sandra Barker
Christopher J. Barlow
E. B. Barmby
J. A. and J. B. Barnaby
Susan and Derek Barnes
Patricia Barrell
Diana, Paul, Joe and Fay Barratt
Wyn Barrett
J. C. A. Barry
Irene Bartlett
Katie Barton
Roy and Norma A. Baskerville
Mrs. C. M. Bates
John Batty
Michael and Dorothy Bayldon
Michael and Margaret Bean
Ian D. Bearpark
Ms Julia Beaumont
A. G. and D. Bell
Janet M. Bell
Margaret Bellis
Robert and Elizabeth Bennett
Mary Berkin
Bertrand and Sheelagh Best
Keith and Cynthia Beverley
Claire Victoria Beverley
Jason Beverley, 15 June 1968
Daniel Beverley, 18 November 1971
Mrs. Joan Bevitt
Anthony and Maxine Bilton

Keith and Betty Binks, South Cave
Ruth and Mark Binny
Alan Binnington
David Binnington
Anne and Allan F. Bird
    Denise, Colin and Abigail Nixey
    Linda Séan and Siân Crotty
    Sarah, Darren, Gemma and A. J.
      Hopper
    Ada Jackson
    Anne and Arthur Thompson
Graham David Bird, 11 July 1956
Mrs. Nora Bird
Mrs. Mabel Birch
Mr. and Mrs. C. S. Blackburn
Mike Blackburn
John W. Blackah
Mrs. Mary Blackwell
Elizabeth A. Blades
Mrs. Jean Blakey
Dennis and Prue Blake
Ruby Bland, B.E.M.
Nigelo Annette Bloomfield
Mrs. P. E. Boatman
Tamar Bolland
Captain and Mrs. R. C. B. Booth
C. R. Bolton
P. J. Boorman
A. Botham
The Bowser Family
Charles Henry Boynton
Geoff and Joan Boynton
John and Christine Bradbury
Andrew Bradley
D. E., D. A. and Matthew Brackenbury
Margaret Brackenbury
Margaret Brammer
Dr. J. F. Branton
David and Jennifer Briggs
Lesley and John Brien and Family
Gerald Broadbent
Ivy B. Broadhurst
Pauline Broadley
Dr. David F. Brook
Alan M. Brooke
    Danielle Farnaby
    Harry Farnaby
Ken and Joan Brooke
Mike and Anne Brookes
Robert G. Brough
Mr. Anthony B. Brough
    Ann M. Martin
Cheryl Brown
Olivia Beatrice Brown

Alan Brown
Mr. Alan E. Brown
Margaret Brown
David Bryce
Bill Bryson and Family
Mrs. E. A. Buck
Paul and Susan Buddery
Roy and Pat Buddery
Erin Kate Buddery
Chelsey and Ellis Buckle
Richard C. Bunting
Des Burdon
Nicola Burke
Peter, Maureen and Lisa Burgess
George Loudon Burns
Walter Laing Burns
Jill R. L. Ellerton Burns
Mr. and Mrs. J. Burrell
David Burrows
Margaret Bush
Mr. and Mrs. J. L. Buxton
Ray and Philip Byrne
Kathleen Byrne
Pat Byass

C
Colin Tara Jamie Cadwallendar
Andrew Maitland Caley
Winnie Cawthorn
E. Calvert
    To Sally Saunders
Peter Calvert
Agnes P. R. Campbell
John D. Carling
Mr. E. T. Carter
Tim Carter
Sheila Carter
Sarah Carter
Caroline Cooper
T. T. Carter
Barbara Sargisson Cartwright
Mrs. H. M. Cartwright
Kathleen Cawston
Mr. and Mrs. G. Cawthorn
Daniel John Chambers
Dr. David G. Chandler
Edward J. Chandler
Margaret and Andrew Chastney
Bob and Hilary Cherry
Mrs. Pam Clark
Tony and Wendy Clark
Mrs. Mary Clay
Mrs. June Cleal
Mr. J. E. Clifton

Mr. and Mrs. A. W. Coates
Ernest Coates
J. and F. Coates
Jennie and Laura Coates
Peter Sydney Coates
Robert E. Cochrane
Muriel Codd
Elizabeth and Raymond Coles
Rebecca and Jamie Coe
The Collins Family
Miss C. M. Cooke
John E. Cooper and Sheila Cooper
Cooper, Peter and Doreen
B. A. Cooper
Monica Joan Cordingley
Zadie and Thomas Cornall
Jim, Joanne, Lynsey and Helen
    Cornfoot
Mr. John Cothill
Carolyn Coupland
Bettie Courts
Mrs. A. Cousins
Thomas Cox
Victoria Cox
Shirley Craft (née) Preston
Philip and Anthea Craggs
Martin Craven
J. L. Crooks
Joyce and Barry Croker
Aline and Roddy Croskin
Margery and Colin Croskin
Mrs. Jean Crowe, Cherry Burton
Mrs. Audrey Crowley
    Mr. Ronald W. Frankish
Jan and Peter Crowther
Malcolm and Gina Cunningham
Gladys Currie
R. A. Curtis
Bob Cuthbertson
Fiona Cuthbertson
Martin Cuthbertson
Caroline Cuthbertson

D
Mrs. Caroline Dainty, from Mum D.
Brian Dalton
Christine Danter
Mrs. Doris Davenport
Steven and Trudi Davidson
Barbara Davie
Mr. D. O. Davis
Miss Margaret C. Davis
Mrs. J. Davison
Martin J. Dawes

D. F. Day
A. G. Day
P. M. Day
Miss M. Dean
Frank Dean
Miss P. E. Deans
Paddy deLacy
A. E. Delaine
Anne and Ken Deighton
Emma and Fiona Delanoy
Dr. George and Mrs. 'Marty' Denning
Dave and Lyn Dennis
Robert Dennis
T. and M. Derenthal
Marie Dicconson
Jill Dickens
Dennis and Barbara Dickinson
Andrew M. Dickinson
Robert E. Dickinson
Mrs. B. Dierckx
Brett Diment
Helen and Les Diment
Gwendoline Ann Dingsdale
Judith Anne Dixon
James Richard Dixon
Janet Dobbie, from Mum
Lesley Pamela Dobson
Jenny Donkin
Stephanie Donkin
Daniel J. Doris
Thomas E. Doris
Peter Doughty
Arthur Douglas
Paul, Bud and Ed Downey
Richard Daniel and Lewis Draper
Michael Driscoll
Ann Drummond
Howard and Allison Dukes
Mabel Dungworth (née Mee)
T. D. D. Dunn, D.F.C.
Mrs. M. J. Dunn
Clive Dunning
Mrs. J. Durham
Nigel and Kathy Dykes
Samuel Dyson

E
Sally and Andy Eastcrabbe
E. M. Edmondson
Mrs. P. M. Elliott
Jonathan Ellis
Chris, Jackie and Rebecca Elvidge
David, Joanne, Cathy and Rob Elwell
Raymond and Jean Elwell

Sheila Endley
Allan English and Pat Lymer
Clifford P. Evans
Sylvia and Peter Everett
James George Evison
Colin E. Ewen
Ed and Serena Ewen, Vanc., Canada

F
Janet and Paul Fairlamb
Maxwell S. Fargus
Mr. and Mrs. Tom Farrell
Mrs. B. Fawcett
Gillian Fawcett
Mrs. Elizabeth Featherstone
R. V. Fenton
Sylvia Ferguson
Pat and Ray Fielden
Joan and Gordon Fielding
Chris Finn and Family
George and Betty Fisher
Ruth Elizabeth Fisher
M. and J. B. Fleming
Doris Fletcher
Harry Patrick Flynn, Hon. Ald.
Mr. Kieran Gregory Flynn
Miss Sheilagh Suzanna Flynn
Peter and Margi Flynn
Anthony and Pat Flynn
Kevin, Carol and Paul Flynn
John, Tracey and Thomas Flynn
Andrew Claire and Kimberley Ford
Ashley Lara Forrest-Curran
J. M. and D. J. Forster
A. and E. K. Foster
John E. Foster
Ron and Jane Foster
Mrs. D. Fox
David William Fox
Mary E. Fox
Ian Alastair Fox
Frank Edwin Fox
Alistair and Joanne Friar
Mr. and Mrs. C. A. Froggatt
Leslie Froomes

G
John Howard Gadd
Shula Galtrey
M. A. Gardham, Sec. Beverley Brass Band
Miss A. M. Gaut
Miss K. L. Gaut
David Marson Gawan-Freeman

Peter H. Gawan-Freeman of Beverley
Mrs. J. A. Gibbard
Andrew, Chris, Becky and Tom Gibbon
George and Yvonne Gibson
Steve and Wendy Gilbank
Mike, Teresa, Emily and Cameron Gill
Lieut. I. M. F. Gillard, M.B.E., J.P., R.N.
M. B. Gilpin
J. P. Gillett
Janice and Norman Gillyon
Mary Glass
Margrét Gledhill
Mr. J. L. Glover
E. A. and M. Godson
Mr. Ian N. Goldthorpe
Kenneth O. M. Golisti
A. B. and S. Golisti
Dr. and Mrs. J. D. Goode
Andrea Goode
Helen Goode
Linda, Trevor and Melissa Grace
Sally Cole, love from Melissa
Patricia Grafton
Sheila Graham
Grantham, R. A., M. P, N. P, D. E.
Harold Gray
Lt.Gen. Sir Michael Gray, K.C.B., O.B.E., D.L.
F. William D. Gray
Cllr. Kate Gray the Mayor 1999/2000
Andrew William Gray
    Sarah Dickinson
Roger and Judy Gray
M. J. Gray
Dick and Betty Gray
Alan Gray
Thomas Abel Gray
Mr. and Mrs. J. R. Grayson
Margaret and Stephen Grayson
The Greatorex Family
Elliot Charles Green
Caroline and Matthew Green (joiner)
Jason and Jayne Green
P. A. Greenwood
Denis Gregory
Fraser, Sarah, Louise and Jessica Gregory
Mollie Gresswell
Jill and Tony Griffin
Peter Griffin
Gina Beverley Griffin
Margaret and John Grimshaw
    Victoria and Geoffrey Norton
Kathryn and Russell Grimshaw

Trish and Simon Grimshaw
Elizabeth Grove
T. J. and J. A. Groves
Michael and Ann Guest
Karen M. Guest
Philip and Helen Guest
Sue Guilford

H
Christine Hagyard
Mr. and Mrs. Ian S. Haigh
Florence Hall
Joan Hall
Lindsay Anne Hall
John and Barbara Hall
Peter and Lydia Hall
Charlie Tyler Moore
Max Lewis Hall
Stephen and Nuala Hall
Duncan and Jan Halliday
W. S. Hamilton
Mr. M. Hancock
Andrew Hancock
Peter Alan Hanmer
Ray and Margaret Harding
Graham Hardy
Mollie and Michael Hardy
James Robert Hardy and Esther Hardy
Janet E. Harlan
Winifred Lee Harper
Gerard Harriott
Digby Harris
C. J. Harrison
Pam and Anthony Harrison
    Mrs. Pat Sprinzl
George R. Hart
Hartley, William and Dorothy
Lynne Margaret Hay
Robert Hatch
Peter I. Hatfield
Adrian Havercroft
Mary P. Hayes
Liz and Anthony Heathcote and Family
Helen Heaton
M. G. and K. Heaton
Peter Hebden
Mrs. Mary Henry
Steve and Heather Heron
Nicola and Matthew Heron
Gabriel Paul Ledraw-Hesp
David Alan Hesp
Steven Edward Hesp
Pat Hewitson
Mrs. Kathleen Hibbert

Jane and George Highmore
Mr. and Mrs. Michael Hildyard
Richard and Victoria Hildyard
J. Hildyard and K. Sutton
D. Hildyard
B. M. and A. M. Hill
David and Joan Hill
C. B. Hinch
Stephen Hird
Christopher Hird
Margaret Hird
Andy Hird
Katie Hird
D. and E. Hirrich
Debra and John Ho, California, U.S.A.
Mr. C. N. and Mrs. L. Hobson
Jonathan and Lindsay Hobson
Charlotte P. A. Hobson
Eleanor S. C. Hobson
Isabel A. M. Hobson
Jayne Hobson
Gavin, Lesley, Jacob and Naomi Hobbs
Kathleen Hogarth
Kathryn Ann Hoggarth
E. A. Holdich
John and Rosaleen Holgate
Karen and Ruarigh Holgate-Dale
Coun. Nev. Holgate
Rodney Holmes
Jim Hood
Philip A. Hood
Peter J. Hood (S. Africa)
Su Hood (U.S.A.)
Alison and Theo Hoppen
Mark, Annette, Chris and Jess Horner
Peter and Kathleen Horrocks
Robert (Bob) Horton
Pamela Hotham
Peter and Nancy Hougham
Captain Edward Howlett
Maureen Howlett
Michael Howlett
Richard and Carol Hudson
Annabel and Jennie Hudson
Mark Hughes
Carol Hunsley
M. and G., J. and M. Hunsley
Alastair and Wendy Hunter
Brenda Hunter
Jim and Sue Hunter
Vanessa Janet Hunter
M. H. Hurst
Mrs. Janet Hutchinson
Mark and Angela Hutchinson

I
Mrs. B. Iddon
Mrs. F. W. Iddon
Valerie M. Illingworth
Mrs. P. Ingleby
Stewart Ireland
John F. Irving

J
David and Nancy Jack
Duncan and Joy Jack
C. Peter Jackson
David G. Jackson
Mabel Jackson
John Rosie and Lucy Jackson
Mr. Stanley Jackson
Mr. and Mrs. W. D. Jackson
Freda, Peter and David Jackson
Dr. Beatrice James
Hugh Edward James
Ruth Eleanor James
Peggy and Bill James
P. M. Jamieson
Mr. and Mrs. J. T. Jenkins
Mary Johnson
Margery Johnston
Pearl and Peter Jolley
Trevor Mostyn Jones, M.B.E.
Bryan and Lilian Jones
Sam John Jones
Alice Mary Jones
Gwyneth M. Jones
Angharad Jones
Caradoc Jones
Mr. and Mrs. G. E. Jones
Mrs. M. Jones
P. I. D. Jones
R. L. Jones
Rhiannon Jones
Sandra J. Jones
Carol Jopling

K
Janet and Richard Kemp
Joan Kemp
J. and A. K. Kennedy
Christopher Ketchell
David Kilford
Janet Kilpatrick
Neil King
Andrew and Debbie Kirkup
Christine and Ron Kirkup
Ian Kirkup
Paul Kirkup

Mr. Raymond Kitching
Katie Marie Knapp
Mrs. M. A. Knowles

L
The Lade Family
Mary and Charles Laing
Brian and Marjorie Lamb
Hugh and Bobbie Lambert
R. A. Landais-Stamp
Mr. and Mrs. G. Lawtey
Mr. and Mrs. R. L. Blockey
Mr. and Mrs A. R. Crisp (Australia)
Mr. and Mrs. P. Laycock
Colin Learie
Mr. P. W. R. Lee
Brian D. Lee
Carolyn Ledgard
Beryl Lee
Enid Leivers
J. B. Leonard
Petr Levitt
Roger Lewis
Richard Lidwell
John G. Lightowler
Abigail Victoria Ling
June and Bill Lockett (Blackpool)
Audrey Locking
Claire Lofthouse
Dave Lofthouse
Mr. Robert Michael Long
Martin Lonsdale
Ian and Diana Long
David Lord
Peter and Ann Los
Wendy Los
Daniel Philip Love
M. Lown
Marjorie A. Lucas
Margaret Jane Lucock
Mr. and Mrs. J. M. Lunn
Mrs. D. Lund
Shirley M. Lyons
Mrs. H. Lythe
Mr. Jeff N. Lyons

M
Stewart MacArthur
Mrs. Irene McArthy
Mrs. Jeanne McBride
Richard McCoid
Michael Julian McDonnell
M. McDonald
To David McGuire

John and Pat McNicholas
Sue Mackie
Mrs. Jean McIlwaine
Rodney W. Mackey
Gordon and Dorothy Mackley
J. K. L. and L. M. Madge
Benjamin, Matthew,Philip, Maher
Rebecca, Geogina, Grace Maher
John Major
Roger and Sally Malton
Peter, Julia and Katherine Mann
Dennis and Gladys Markham
John Markham
Tony Markham
    Peter and Christine Cole
Andrew Marr
Keith Marriott
Mrs. Patricia Zoe Marshall-Lagar
Mrs. Hazel Marshall-Palmer
Geoff and Maureen Marson
Mrs. J. P. Martin
Tom and Anne Martin
Angela M. Martinson
Basil Mason
Derrick and Brenda Massey
May Matthews
Mick and Ann Mawer
Betty Mawson (née Franklin)
Mrs. Margaret E. Mayne
Jean and Ron Medley
Dr. Edvardo Mendez
Mrs. Patricia Ann Mercer
Laura Faith Meredith
Renato and Clarisse Merolli
Giulia Grezzana Merolli
Sophie and Nicholas Metcalfe
Mrs. June Middleton
Des and Christine Milburn
Miss Caroline Milledge, B.Sc.
Mrs. Miller
Miss E. D. Millest
Lucy and Paul Milner
Terri Milner
Laura May Minnikin
Ben Anthony Minnikin
Mrs. Audrey Mitchell
Gillian E. Mitchell
Mr. and Mrs. J. T. Mitchell
Margaret and Don Mitchell
R. W. and J. E. Mitchell
Margery Moffat
Keith and Berna Moody
Joyce and Mike Moore
Miss Norah Moore

Dora and Cliff Morgan
Mr. and Mrs. F. G. Morrill and Family
Brian and Bess Morris
Charles, Alison and Katie Morris
A. B. Moverley
Eva Muff (née Johnson)
Ida Watt (née Johnson)
Paul, Karyn and Rose Murby
David P. Musgrave
Andrew D. Myers
Claire I. Myers
Frank Myers

N
David and Susan Neave
Dorothy Nelson
Mervin and Sue Nethercoat
Mrs. Margaret Newbould
Mark, Sylvia, Carla and Sophie Nicholson
Peter Gawan and Jean Nicholson
Timothy M. Nicholson
Suzie J. Nicholson
Edward and Anita Norman
Thomas Norris
Sylvia Norton
Hilary Nowell
C. Kent Nowell
Jilla and Kent Nowell
The Nye Family

O
Simon and Cath O'Connor and Family
Mrs. G. R. Odey
Christine and Harry Oglesby
Bill and Georgina Oldfield
Susan Oliver
Yvonne Oliver
Reg and Vera Osgerby
Jessie D. Oston
Colin Otter
C. Oxtoby
Faith D. Oxtoby
Owen Oxtoby

P
Kevin and Debbie Padget
Barbara Parham
Dennis and Angela Parker
Margaret and Stanley Parker
R. and J. Parkinson
S. Parkinson
Mr. and Mrs. P. Peacock
R. R. and J. M. Pearcy
Jane Pearson – Artist

Lesley and Walter Pearson
Roland G., Jane L. and Sarah L. Peck
Mrs. Freda Pegg
Victoria Petty
Joyce Phillips
Graham and Linda Phoenix
Mrs. C. D. Platt
Doreen Plews
Sylvia Yvonne Plews
Sheila Pickering
Mr. T. J. Pickering
Joan Pillmoor
C. A. and J. Pinder
Cora Pinder and Family
John Dudley Pitts
Gareth D. Winkle and B. M. Place
F. W. Plaster
Alan and Trish Porter
Ronald and Barbara Prather, U.S.A.
Guy Preston
Joan Price
L. A. and R. Proctor
Gary Matthew Proud
P. F. L. Purser

R
Terence G. Railton
Don, Leslie, Mark and Stephen Raine
Bill and Mary Rambold, V.A.1 Canada
David and Henrietta Ramsay and
    Family
Guy and Diana Randle
Mrs. Jacqueline Rank
Peter and Carole Ranson
Trevor and Pauline Ranson
Brian and Janet Rawcliffe
Mr. and Mrs. K. A. Rawcliffe
J. E. Ream
A. Stothard
Bridget and David Reason
A. Redhead
Margaret Redmond
M. E. Rhodes
Margaret Rice
Bill Rice
Kitson Saul Richardson
Fred, Elsie and Stephen Richardson
Jennifer Anne Richardson
Joanne Richardson
Raymond Mansfield Richardson
Patricia Riggs
Sylvia Ripley
Christine and Brian Rippingale
Gertrude M. Rispin

Mrs. M. S. Rispin
William Robert Risso-Gill
Sofia Lily Risso-Gill
Myles and Nina Ritson
Christine Roberts
Stephen P. Roberts
Ann, Harry, Lisa and Philip Robinson
Charles Dobbie Robinson
David and Jane Robinson
Mrs. E. Robinson
Bas and Carole Robinson
Paul Robinson
Peter Robinson
Wendy Robinson
Shirley Robinson
Kay Robins
Mr. and Mrs. Gordon H. Robson
Sue and Steve Robson
Megan Elizabeth Rodgers
Joe and June Roe
William Ross
    Vera Smith (Ross)
Allan and Carol Rowlands
Simon Lee Rowlands
    Avril Marie Hiles
Lillian Olive White (née Good)
Jennifer C. Rowley
Mark Julian Ruston
Andrew James Ruston
David Rutherfoord
Joseph John Ryane 1926
Diane Ryland
Gladys Rylatt

S
Nigel Salt
Mr. A. R. C. Sanctuary
Mrs. J. M. Sanctuary
Edward Sayers
Geoffrey and Jennifer Scaife
    Karen and John 25th Anniversary
David Veronica and Jen Scrimger
Kenneth Scruton
Miss Ruby Seager
Clive H. Searby
P. C. and J. Searby
John and Marjory Searl
Alexandra Jayne Seaton
Michael James Sellen-Metcalf
Eleanor May Sellen-Metcalf
I. H. and J. Schofield
Elizabeth Rachel Sharpe 1990
Rob, Pauline, Rachel and Amanda Shaw
The Shaw Family

Jayne Shepherd
E. and J. M. Shepherdson
P. R. J. Sheppard
Kathryn F. Sheridan
Malcolm Shields
Alan and Julie Shingles
Ben Shires
Diana Shutt
Clare Shutt
Gilly and Brenda Sibert
Albert and Doreen Sidebottom
Noel and Mary Siddy
Ted Skelton
John Edward Skinner
Andrew Skinner
Joe and Betty Smales, Ont., Canada
George D. Smedley
Malcolm and Marion Smiles
Mr. and Mrs. Peter Smith and Family
Brenda Smith and Graham Edward Smith
Mr. A. and Mrs. B. Smith
Mr. and Mrs. Bernard Smith
Elizabeth Smith
Mrs. Margaret Smith
Molly I. Smith
P. K. and A. Smith
Robert P. Smith
S. K. Smith
Yvonne Smith
Mr. and Mrs. W. W. Smith
W. W. Smith, F.C.A.
Vera Snowden
Mrs. Marilyn A. Soanes
Clifford and Pauline Soule
J. E. Spencer
Gerald and Valerie Spinks
Harold Stabeler
Anne and Martin Stainsby
Colin and Shiela Stamford
Mick and Gill Stanley
Mrs. Helga Stephens
Mr. and Mrs. G. M. Stephenson
Hilary A. Stephenson
Hannah C. Stephenson
W. E. Stephenson
Mrs. Audrey Stevens
H. J. Salton
Jennifer A. Stewart
H. and M. I. Stickney
Sarah Stocks
Joyce Storr
Pauline Storr
Yorkshire Yankees – Susan and Gary
    Stoh

J. C. Stothard
The Stout Family
Dorothy Stutt
Joseph Brian and Valerie Sutton
David Allen Sutton
Paul Shaw Sutton
Karen Heather Sutton
Mrs. M. Swales (née Goulding)
Mr. Iain Richard Swallow
Geoffrey Swan
Graham Sweeney

T
Sharan Carol Harness (née Tanton)
Susan Carmel Grassby (née Tanton)
H. P. Tate, B.A.
Cath Tattersall
Arthur and Enid Taylor
John and Lesley Taylor
Richard, Rebecca and Kate Taylor
Winifred M. Taylor
Mr. and Mrs. D. Templeman
Thirsk, James Wood
Mrs. Jean Blackburn (née Thirsk)
Betty Thirsk
Mrs. Sue Thomas
Chris and Jenny Thompson
Garry Alvin Thompson
Irene Thompson
Jill Thompson
Beryl and Ron Thomson
Mrs. M. C. Thorogood
John L. Thorpe
John Pat Adam Michael Toes
Peter William David Tomkys
Alan and Lucy Tovey
Peter and Jane Duffield
Sue and Des Townsend
Mrs. Eileen Towse
G. and E. Tracy
Siân Troote
Fay Troote
Masters A. M. and N. Try
Colin and Joyce Try
Jenny Pick (Try)
Gillie Davies (Try)
Jane Brown (Try)
Chris Try
Lesley Tucker
Richard Tucker and Melanie Shane
John and Ruth Tunnicliffe
Clive and Ann Turgoose
Adele Turner
The Rev'd. Carl Francis Turner

Vera Turner (née Willey)
Carol Turner
John Irwin Turner
Sarah J. Tyrrell

U
Miss M. S. Uncles
Stephen W. Upton
Alex and Jo Urquhart
Ivan, Hilary and Gregory Usher
Rod Usher
Jennifer M. Uttley

V
Mr. and Mrs. John Veall
Mrs. Alicia Viant
Paul Vinsen

W
To Zac Wade, love Nanna and Pappa
Rene and Brian Wald
Ann Eleanor Walker
Chris Walker, Pasture Freeman
Mary Walker
Professor Ray Walker
Mr. Neil and Mrs. Rachael Walker
Mrs. Nina Walker
Susan E. Walker
William Thomas Walker
Tom and Barbara Waller
W. A. Walsh
J. M. and E. M. Ward
Betty and Ray Ward
Ward, Leslie Geoffrey
Robert and Joyce Ward
Wendy Wardropper
Stuart Warner
Adam Waterhouse
Mr. and Mrs. J. A. Waterworth
Bernard and Marie Watson
Mr. C. K. Watson
Joanne Watson
F. H. Watts
Angela and John Wells
Tony and Sylvia Wells
Everill West
Hon. Alderman Doreen E. West
Michaela J. West
Stephen and Sarah West
John, Margaret, Colin and Claire
    Weston
John and Lilian Woodward
Shirley Westra
Michael John Wheatley

Bridget Maria Parr
Clare Frances Wheatley
David and Collette White
Jane White
Thomas Dean Whitehead
Mrs. Margaret Anne Whitehead
'Major' Whitehead
David and Ann Whittaker
Clive Widdall
John Wigglesworth
Amanda, Roger and Reuben Wilde
Patricia Wiles
Mr. Arthur Wilkinson
Carole Wilkinson
Doreen Wilkinson
I. D. Wilkinson
John and Joyce Wilkinson
Philip and Tina Wilkinson
Andrew Vincent Wilks
Hannah Frances Willingham
Rosalind Willoughby
B. J. and N. Wilson
Carenza Wilson
Dianne Wilson
Dorothy Wilson
E. and R. Wilson
Jane and Gregor Wilson
Jean Wilson
Ros Legg
Kate, Richard, Dan, Toby, and Oli
    Wilson
Michael A. Wilson
Brenda and Roy Wilson
Professor John Wilton-Ely
    Valerie R. Thornhill
Kathy and Tony Wise
J. A. and P. M. Wollaston
Janet Wood
Mr. and Mrs. A. E. Wood
Mrs. Sandra Wood
Mr. Simon Wood
Peter and June Woodcock
John and Tina Woodcock
Anne Woodfield
Madge Woolf (née Robinson)
Jacqueline Ann Wormald
Mark Woollven
David Wray
E. W. Wright
Fiona Wright
Dominic Wright
Colin Wright
Jane and Paul Wright

BEVERLEY
A Portrait of a Town at the Millennium

In 1991 Neil King, Secretary of the Beverley and District Civic Society, announced a plan for sponsored floodlighting of the Minster. For a payment of £15 an individual or organisation could select a night for floodlighting – which transforms the great church into a spiritual beacon as the Second Millennium ends and the Third begins.

St. Mary's Church, viewed from the corner of Wood Lane. Originally a chapel of ease for the convenience of Beverlonians as the town grew in a northerly direction away from the Minster, it developed as a parish church in its own right. Its strong musical tradition, the participation of parishioners in a whole variety of activities and organisations (aided by the opening of a new church hall) make it a lively community church with a great influence on the life of Beverley.

Beverley from the tower of St. Mary's Church, with Ladygate at the bottom right.

St. Nicholas' Church.

2

CHURCHES

The Millennium celebrations mark the 2,000th anniversary of the start of the Christian era and it is, therefore, only right that this book should begin with churches. Beverley has had a long history as a town in which religion has been a powerful force. Its very origin is associated with the saint who chose to spend his years of retirement here. But after being a great Catholic centre in the Middle Ages, Beverley turned strongly Protestant after the Reformation, though one of its sons, John Fisher, became the town's second saint through his opposition to Henry VIII. At the Second Millennium there are many complaints about falling church attendances, but sectarian rivalries have virtually disappeared, and the different denominations have never worked more closely or in a friendlier spirit, strong indications that the Christian message is properly understood and put into practice: a hopeful sign for a future which is certain to be vastly different from the past.

The west towers of the Minster, impressive from any angle; here viewed from Minster Yard North.

Beverley Minster bell-ringers (Captain, Mike Robson), who 'make as joyful a sound' at their Wednesday practices as they do on Sundays and at weddings.

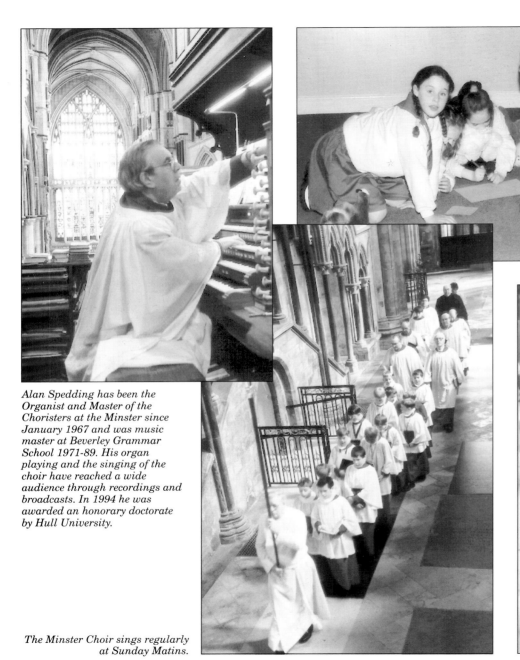

Alan Spedding has been the Organist and Master of the Choristers at the Minster since January 1967 and was music master at Beverley Grammar School 1971-89. His organ playing and the singing of the choir have reached a wide audience through recordings and broadcasts. In 1994 he was awarded an honorary doctorate by Hull University.

The Minster Choir sings regularly at Sunday Matins.

The wedding of Grace Godfrey and David Carlin at the Minster, 3 April 1999.

Top Centre – The 2nd Beverley Minster Brownie Guide Pack, which is run by Mrs. Wendy Gilbank, enjoying a teddy bears' picnic on 26 March 1999.

Flower arranging is now an extremely popular artistic activity and most churches make a great feature of their floral displays. Here Easter flowers are arranged in the Minster

The nave of the Minster looking east towards the magnificent organ and the altar beyond.

A great annual event, the service to commemorate St. John of Beverley, held on the Sunday nearest to the anniversary of his death 7 May 721 – here on 9 May 1999.

The East Riding County Choir at their annual Christmas concert in the Minster on 4 December 1998. The choir was founded in 1958 and has been conducted by Alan Spedding since 1969. Concerts are given on the first Saturdays in May and December. (Courtesy Hull Daily Mail)

Distant views of the Minster enable it to be seen in its splendid entirety. This view is from Victoria Road, once rural, but in recent years an area of massive housing development.

Global warming has made the severe winters of the past a rarity, but enough snow fell for this photograph to be taken.

Left and right – St. Mary's Garden Party, held in the church because of rain on Saturday, 27 June 1998. In 1999 it was decided to replace the traditional garden party with an open day on 26 June.

Bottom left – Beverley Chamber Choir, founded in July 1998 by Alan Binnington. In 1999 it performed in three northern cathedrals, Ripon, Sheffield and York.

4th Beverley St. Mary's Guide Unit (Leader Joy Billany) and
4th Beverley St. Mary's Brownie Guide Pack (Leader Julia French).

Decorating St. Mary's Church for Christmas 1998. Mrs. Dorothy Mackley.

Above right – St. Mary's decorated in readiness for the Christmas Carol Service 1998.

Kneelers in St. Michael's Chapel, St. Mary's Church, made as part of the Millennium celebration scheme for the refurbishment of the chapel. All are to the same design – a Celtic cross with '2000' across the centre. On the underside are the names of the donor, the worker and a dedication.

4th Beverley St. Mary's Guide Unit and 4th Beverley St. Mary's Brownie Guide Pack .

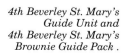

The Church Lads Brigade, a name redolent of its time, was the pride and joy of its founder, Neville Hobson, Beverley solicitor and great public figure, who created the organisation in 1908. Now renamed Church Lads and Church Girls Brigade, led by Graham Downing, they are seen marching to the service to mark their 91st anniversary on 18 April 1999, and arriving at St. Mary's. Christopher N. Hobson, son of Neville, watches the entry (top r.)

St. Nicholas Church, the Victorian church built to replace the original building which fell into disrepair and was finally demolished in the 17th century. Children from St. Nicholas School celebrate their harvest festival, October, 1998, gifts later being distributed to the ill and elderly.

Bottom left – St. Mary's floodlit, Christmas 1998.

1st Beverley St. Nicholas Scouts, led by Harry Oglesby, in the old parish hall, Holmechurch Lane.

Mrs. Betty Gray arranging memorial lilies in St. Mary's, Easter 1999.

9

St. John of Beverley Catholic Church. The present building was first used in December 1897; soon after its centenary a major programme of alterations was started.

St. John of Beverley Catholic Church. During restoration.

St. John of Beverley Catholic Church. After completion of the work. The church was consecrated, for the first time, by Bishop John Crowley, 7 May 1999.

Work in progress on the Parish Hall, with scaffolding on the church.

Toll Gavel United Church, originally the Wesley Church, acquired its present name in 1976 after it was united with worshippers from the former United Reformed Church, Lairgate. Many people call in for refreshments, and the church's premises are used for a variety of meetings, both religious and secular.

The simple modern Quaker Meeting House, opened 1961 in Quaker Lane off Woodlands, not far from an earlier Meeting House.

Toll Gavel United Church.
Children's Nativity play, 13 December 1998.

Toll Gavel United Church.
A concert on 7 March 1999 by Beverley Male Voice Choir, founded 1955 by Bob Carr and now conducted by Ian Brocklesby.

No formal service is held, and members and attenders meet in silence and share silent or vocal ministry as the Spirit moves. All are free to speak.

Flemingate Methodist Church, built 1881-2 to replace an earlier one in Blucher Lane.

Norwood Methodist Church – the present church was added in 1901 to a building opened in 1881.

Salvation Army Officer, Chris Broadley, regularly seen in Toll Gavel selling The War Cry.

Latimer Memorial (Congregational) Church, Grovehill Road, built 1934-5 to replace the Shepherd Memorial Mission Chapel ('the tin tabernacle').

The Church of Latter Day Saints, Manor Road, opened 1964.

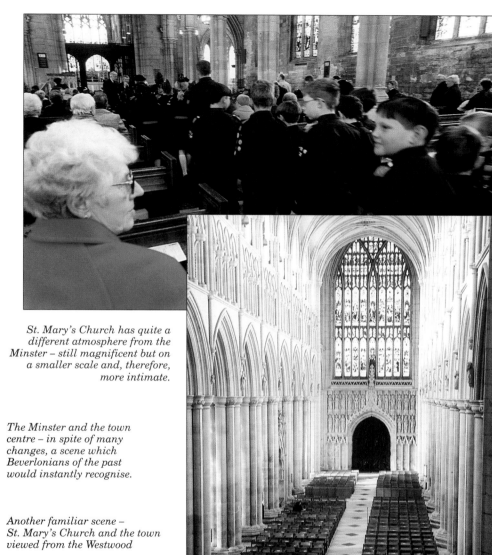

St. Mary's Church has quite a different atmosphere from the Minster – still magnificent but on a smaller scale and, therefore, more intimate.

The Minster and the town centre – in spite of many changes, a scene which Beverlonians of the past would instantly recognise.

Another familiar scene – St. Mary's Church and the town viewed from the Westwood

The nave of the Minster – built in the 14th century in the Decorated style and probably looking as splendid as it has ever done.

Children of St. Nicholas' Junior School at
their Harvest Festival in St. Nicholas'
Church. 20 October 1998.

Saturday Market – flower stall on Corn Hill,
the southern section of Saturday Market.

5th Beverley Wesley Rainbows
at Toll Gavel United Church.
Organiser – Mrs. S. Marin.

Saturday Market charity stall near the
Market Cross – this is available to local
organisations wishing to raise funds.

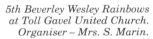

THE TOWN

'Beverley isn't what it was,' is heard every day, and older people look nostalgically back to a time when the town was smaller, traffic lighter and shops were all long-established family businesses. Anyone flicking through this section would have to agree that the changes of the last century have been profound, with familiar sights disappearing, old buildings taking on new uses and, above all, the massive increase in traffic for which the streets were never intended. But change is nothing new. The Georgians could be ruthless in destroying such landmarks as Keldgate Bar and Newbegin Bar, while Beverley's much admired 18th- and 19th-century buildings replaced ones which were older and more traditional. What matters is managing change, so that the best of the past is retained and only the worst is replaced by something better.

The Millennium finds the Sessions House, New Walk, in a state of limbo.
Built 1808-10 and originally used for the Quarter Sessions, it later became a Crown Court. The Lord Chancellor's Department has given up its lease and at the present time it lies abandoned, awaiting an uncertain future.

North Bar Without, the road from North Bar, which becomes New Walk and later Molescroft Road, is probably the most favoured residential area in Beverley. The current passion for all things Georgian has raised the value of the houses of that period.

Although Beverley no longer has racing stables – or coaching inns – it retains its historic character as a horsey town through its races and the current popularity of riding. Horses from Joyce Fern's stables in Bleach Yard, New Walk, are a frequent sight on their way to the Westwood.

New Walk – originally a rural lane, with later infilling of houses, and now a select residential area, though complaints are made about the number of cars parked there since parking fees were introduced into the town centre.

Below left – Regulations no longer permit buses and lorries to – attempt to – pass under the low-arched North Bar, though occasionally large vehicles still become stuck when drivers fail to observe the rules.

NORTH BAR
THIS BAR IS THE ONLY REMAINING ONE OF THOSE WHICH FORMERLY GUARDED THE MAIN ENTRANCES TO THE TOWN. IT WAS BUILT BY THE TOWN COUNCIL IN 1409 AT A COST OF £96-0-1¼.

The Red House, one of the larger houses in North Bar Without (No. 56) dates from 1765. It is now subdivided into flats.

The Rose and Crown's 'Tudor' half-timbering is 20th-century and was added when the main entrance was moved to the side facing North Bar Without from the increasingly busy York Road. The area at the front had been occupied by shops. Now famous for its floral displays and the quality and quantity of its bar meals.

The Royal Standard, North Bar Within, popular with both regulars and visitors and noted for its colourful displays of flowers.

Below left – North Bar Within – now more a shopping than a residential area, with quality shops and a lively atmosphere.

Below right – The former Georgian coaching inn, the Tiger, 43 North Bar Within, has been converted into specialist shops.

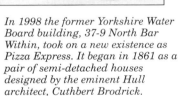

In 1998 the former Yorkshire Water Board building, 37-9 North Bar Within, took on a new existence as Pizza Express. It began in 1861 as a pair of semi-detached houses designed by the eminent Hull architect, Cuthbert Brodrick.

35 North Bar Within – built around 1740 by Beverley builder-architect, William Wrightson, it is now the premises of Quick & Clarke, estate agents.

After lying empty for a considerable time and the subject of much controversy as its four-acre garden was a surviving major green space in central Beverley, St. Mary's Manor re-opened in 1999, converted into ten luxury apartments (upper right).

Rear extension of St. Mary's Manor containing 30 apartments. In the grounds have been built homes for the elderly, a mental health care rehabilitation unit and houses under a shared ownership scheme (lower right).

The Beverley Arms, formerly the Blue Bell and rebuilt 1794-6, was sold by Trust House Forte to Regal Hotels in 1996 and underwent major internal alterations 1998-9.

More and more packaging, fast-foods and take-aways mean constant work for street cleaners. Beverley's 'green machine' – here at work outside the Beverley Arms.

A vivid example of an increasing problem at the end of the Second Millennium. Here a pantechnicon turns into Hengate, posing a danger of structural damage by vibration to St. Mary's Church.

Below – Paul and Robert Simson of Simson's Pet Shop and Photographers.

Right – St. Mary's east end viewed from Memorial Gardens in Hengate.

A site awaiting its next phase. In 1840 a large public hall was erected at the rear of the Georgian Assembly Rooms and in 1935 the building was converted into the Regal Cinema and ballroom (r.). Films ceased to be shown in 1968 and the building, latterly a nightclub, was empty from 1998, awaiting development or demolition (below right). After much controversy permission was given for demolition and there are plans to build a public house and apartments on the site.

Memorial Gardens, Hengate, created on land given by Clive Wilson in 1917 which had formerly been occupied by his home, Church House, destroyed by fire on 29 December 1912.

Hengate has some interesting buildings but is not equipped for modern traffic, even though a one-way system is in operation. The White Horse ('Nellie's') (right background) is as popular as ever, particularly as a venue for folk music.

Crown Mews, officially described as 'almshouses' but in reality excellent modern accommodation for elderly people, skilfully converted by Beverley Consolidated Charities from the former Crown Brushworks and opened by Lady Benson on 1 December 1998.

The White Horse, Hengate, the most famous pub in Beverley – and even well-known internationally – is still affectionately called 'Nellie's' after its late proprietor Miss Nellie Collinson. Although alterations have been made since the Collinson era, it retains its distinctive atmosphere. It is now the venue of a flourishing folk club.

Norwood House – another important building awaiting its fate at the Millennium. A distinguished Georgian residence, converted for use by Beverley High School in 1908, now suffers from dry rot which is estimated will cost over £° million to eradicate.

Globe Mews – named after the Globe Inn, demolished as part of the scheme to create Sow Hill Road and New Walkergate: a good example, of the revival of a residential town centre with well-designed housing.

The car park, Morton Lane, now the focus of much attention with plans for a supermarket pending.

A rear entrance to Globe Mews, still known in Beverley by the traditional, inexplicable – and probably unique – name of 'racket'.

The building of Sow Hill Road allowed buses to be moved from the increasingly crowded Saturday Market to this new bus station with access from New Walkergate.

Tymperon House, Old Walkergate, originally one of the alms houses donated by philanthropic Georgians – in this case created by William Tymperon c1731 – for six elderly women and a matron; now a private house

When the building of New Walkergate was under consideration in the 1970s, critics argued that it would become a race track cutting the town in two. Their worst fears have not been fulfilled, but the quantity of traffic certainly makes pedestrian crossings essential.

Jacob's Well, Ladygate, a charity founded by Dr. Beryl Beynon, has given great help to people in distress in poorer countries.

Ladygate, a useful link between Hengate and Saturday Market, and a minor version of York's Shambles, fell into serious decline in the post-war period but survived all threats of demolition and has not only been preserved but attractively upgraded. Below – the northern end.

Swaby's Yard – Outhouses in a carrier's yard have been converted into a pleasant courtyard with shops and a café (in the former Scotch Baptist Chapel of 1808).

North Bar Within on the main route to York, Driffield and the coast, has always been a busy and attractive part of Beverley with its inns, shops and up-market businesses, and is now very popular with tourists.

Copperfields Bistro 22, 22 North Bar Within. Providing meals, snacks, bar meals and fast foods has become an important part of Beverley's economy. In the past the street was regarded as a place of trade, but there have been complaints that signs are an obstruction to pedestrians. Yorkshire Puddings are as popular as ever, but fish and chips are probably the national dish.

Newly erected houses in Wood Lane. The neo-Georgian style is popular in a town which has so many buildings of the Georgian period. Bricks, the traditional building material in Beverley, have come back into vogue.

Old and new: Old Waste between Saturday Market and Lairgate is a piece of ground which, as its name implies, has never been occupied by buildings, but a significant change is that in 1999 the Midland Bank became the HSBC [Hongkong and Shanghai Banking Company].

Careful restoration still in progress on shops on the east side of North Bar Within, which forms part of the designated conservation area.

The Cross Keys, Lairgate, another Georgian coaching inn, now very popular with young people and used as a meeting venue by various organisations.

Saturday Market – Beverley's commercial centre – and a car park except on Saturdays.

In spite of traffic Newbegin retains its character as a Georgian backwater with attractive well-designed houses.

Shops on Sow Hill.

A wedding at the Register Officer, Lairgate, 30 January 1999, between Christopher Conroy and Irene Oaten.

George Fairfield, a man who has had a very varied career and has worked at the Beverley Arms for many years. Now in his 89th year, he is seen tending his flower baskets at the hotel.

The Spring hat collection in The Hat Box, Dyer Lane; proprietor Ann Booth.

Police car in Saturday Market. Conditions can be rather different late on Friday and Saturday evenings.

Beverley Garland Dancers at the Folk Festival, 19 June 1998.

Beverley has a long tradition as a military town. Here the Army recruiting in Saturday Market.

The start of the East Riding of Yorkshire Classic Cycle Race organised by the Hull Thursday Road Club, 25 April 1999. The race, covering 155 miles in three stages over two days, was won by Gethin Butler of London.

Police horses from the Walkington stables are a regular and popular sight in the centre of Beverley.

Looking from Saturday Market to North Bar Within.

Above right – Shops on Saturday Market in the area known as Butterdings after the nearby 'Butter Cross', where farmers' wives once sold their produce.

The Push, Corn Hill, was for years unofficially so named because of the sign on its door: now it bears the name proudly. Next door the 1886 Corn Exchange, now The Picture Playhouse, providing films and live entertainment; under restoration at the time of this photograph.

The Green Dragon's central location and the increased flexibility of licensing hours bring it all-day trade. At the rear is another new popular facility, a beer garden.

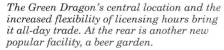

Beverley traffic problems at the Millennium.
A huge delivery van in Saturday Market,

and, below, a security van at Lloyds Bank.

Bottom left – Habbershaws, the Beverley
branch of a well-known firm of bookmakers,
35 Saturday Market. New legislation and the
opening of betting shops has made the illegal
'bookie's runner' a thing of the past.

Saturday Market stalls link modern Beverley to the times when more trading was done in the streets. The type of goods has changed, but the idea of a bargain accompanied by Yorkshire humour remains as strong as ever.

Saturday Market provides more than a chance to shop. It is a social occasion, a place where you are almost guaranteed to meet someone you know, and an attraction for people from a wide surrounding area.

The King's Head, Saturday Market – a Georgian inn which has moved with the times, building up a reputation for its catering and expanding into adjacent premises.

The 'barker' selling meat at bargain prices has become a familiar, if ear-splitting, feature of the Sow Hill section of the Saturday Market.

Burgess's, still the local name for ice-cream.

The Alfresco Bistro – Fast food has gained enormous popularity in recent years. During term, Toll Gavel is crowded with pupils who prefer snacks to school dinners – and with those who 'graze' at all times of the day.

'Bim' Pougher, fishmonger, previously had shops in Saturday Market and Cross Street.

Stalls on Corn Hill.

Saturday Market at night. A late 20th-century problem, by no means restricted to Beverley, is the fear of going out after dark because of possible violence. The likelihood of such an incident is rare but the nervousness remains.

Newbegin House – described on television by architectural expert Alec Clifton-Taylor as Beverley's finest house; built c1689 for Charles Warton, a member of an influential Beverley family.

Lairgate – four bede houses, Lairgate, an example of Beverley Consolidated Charities' older almshouses, founded at least by the 17th century, rebuilt in 1862 – and still in use.

The Hall, Lairgate. An 18th-century house once known as Pennyman House after its early owners, later the home of the Walker family and still sometimes called Admiral Walker Hall after its last private occupant who died in 1925; it then became the property of Beverley Borough Council. Recently, amid much controversy, it was sold to Bramley Holdings.

Toll Gavel – west side.

Toll Gavel, Beverley's main thoroughfare, pedestrianised in 1982, and usually bustling. In a town of fine architecture Beverley has some disappointingly mediocre buildings in its main street.

Toll Gavel – now that it is pedestrianised, street traders and entertainers create a colourful scene, particularly on Saturdays.

Toll Gavel – east side.

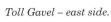

Toll Gavel – looking south from its junction with Cross Street.

Always fascinating – the snakes on the former apothecary's shop (now Jumpers) – but heads have had to be replaced after vandalism.

Landress Lane (looking from Toll Gavel) still residential but also a pleasant shopping mall.

Toll Gavel – looking north from its junction with Cross Street.

A modern shop sign – Dynasty, 1 Cross Street – obviously a shoe shop.

A typical Beverley story. Modern shops on the ground floor of Georgian buildings in Cross Street.

Register Square – the 18th-century Guildhall, for long the home of Beverley Borough Council, it passed to the newly created East Riding of Yorkshire Council in 1996. The new Beverley Town Council, elected 1999, has requested its use as headquarters, but at the time of writing this has been refused, though it is to be allowed to hold its meetings in the building.

Post Office, Register Square, now re-organised as Post Office Counters Ltd. and offering a wide range of services which would astound Rowland Hill, the 19th-century pioneer of the penny post.

This junction of Toll Gavel, Butcher Row and Old Walkergate is a key to Beverley's development. The bend of Old Walkergate follows the course of the stream (now culverted) which started in the north of the town. The street where cloth was 'walked' in the cleaning and shrinking process grew up on its bank. The bridge with the chapel (later a lock-up) has gone, but the outline of 'Prison Pump' is still – just – visible on the shop, Country Concept (for many years the premises of Marson and Wood's shoe shop).

Toll Gavel – the southern section which becomes Butcher Row at its junction with Old Walkergate

Butcher Row.

Pavers being taken up at the junction of Old Walkergate and Butcher Row, to be replaced by brick setts.

The Foneshop, Butcher Row. Both spelling and merchandise are significant features of late 20th-century life. Americanisation and advertising have been strong influences on the English language, and technology has made mobile phones an everyday sight in Beverley streets.

The Angel, kept in the 19th century by the legendary Liberal landlord – and briber – Daniel Boyes, has a pleasant atmosphere which appeals to tourists as well as its regulars.

Butcher Row looking north from Wednesday Market.

Well Lane.

Wednesday Market – Relaying brick setts, January 1999. Beverley's oldest market area declined as Saturday Market developed, and closed in the 18th century.
History has now turned full circle, with stalls in Wednesday Market on Wednesdays, and an overflow from Saturday Market on Saturdays.

Wednesday Market – The focus is now on tourism and leisure, and Beverley attracts visitors from home and abroad.

Butcher Row in summer.

Ye Olde Pork Shoppe, Wednesday Market, (still with the bracket of the sign when it was the Spotted Cow) is a traditional family business with many regular customers who appreciate personal service and a chance to chat. Proprietors: brothers John and Christopher Hillman.

Below left – Beverley Library (ground floor) and Art Gallery (first floor). Originally run by Beverley Borough Council, later by Humberside County Council and now by the East Riding of Yorkshire Council, the Library, opened in 1906, has kept pace with modern developments, particularly technological. The Art Gallery, for too long dismal and drab, has been considerably improved, offering temporary exhibitions as well as its important collection of paintings by F. W. Elwell.

The neat and dignified frontage of Boyes' store, Wednesday Market, has received deserved praise – particularly as it has replaced an unlovely garage.

People are living longer and the demand for accommodation for the elderly has grown. Many residential homes are privately run, but Minster Towers is run by the local authority.

Saturday Market looking to St. Mary's from the top of Beverley Building Society.

Saturday Market from Sow Hill Road (a new road of the late 1960s).

Winters have become much milder but a fall of snow has enhanced the appearance of the Sow Hill part of Saturday Market.

Beverley Beck, no longer a commercial waterway, has taken on a new lease of life as a leisure amenity – and new houses are changing the appearance of the old industrial area.

A regular scene in modern Beverley – removing the rubbish skip.

A welcome type of traffic – an electrically operated chair – here driven by Michael Appleby.

Advertising in Sow Hill Road.

Another sign of progress – ready-mixed concrete delivered direct to the door.

Highgate (looking north) – probably Beverley's best Georgian street (though complaints are still made about the demolition of a half-timbered house and the intrusion of modern flats) leading to the most used entrance to the Minster.

Eastgate – usually very busy with traffic from and to Hull passing uncomfortably close to the Minster. Beverley still awaits the completion of a full encirclement of by-passes.

Ann Routh's Almshouses, Keldgate – named after their founder, a Georgian philanthropist, their provision of separate accommodation for elderly females and now elderly gentlemen supervised by a warden, is in line with modern ideas on retaining independence in old age.

The Grammar Schoolmaster's House, Keldgate. The school had moved around the town before settling in Queensgate in 1902: originally at the Minster it was in Keldgate by c1816, then in Albert Terrace.

Beverley Station. The coming of the railway in 1846 was the start of Beverley's new role as a commuter town. Although there have been periodic threats to this coastal line, the section between Hull and Beverley, much used because of its convenience, surely makes it safe. On privatisation, 2 March 1997, the line was taken over by Regional Railways North East. The name was changed to Northern Spirit on 21 May 1998.

Station booking office. Current arrangements for buying tickets will no doubt one day be a historical curiosity.

The station was refurbished in 1993, with further alterations made after complaints by conservationists.

The Dominican Friary – in the 1960s the subject of heated discussion when its future was in doubt. Beverley Minster had sold it to Armstrong Patents, which extended its factory up to the Friary and wanted to demolish it. The Beverley Friary Preservation Trust was founded, the Friary was saved and restored, and, after various ideas were mooted, eventually became an excellent Youth Hostel in 1984. It has public rooms separate from the hostel.

Pedestrian bridge in the station.

– with its view of the signal box and the housing development in Eastgate.

Flemingate railway crossing. From its earliest days there were complaints about the number of crossings needed on this line. Fines on drivers who try to beat the lights have not proved a total deterrent.

The closure of Armstrong Patent's Eastgate factory in 1981 freed a large site for successful conversion into an attractive residential area, with smart town houses and accommodation for the elderly provided by Joseph Rowntree Housing Trust. Names given to streets in this area are a reminder of the site's early history.

Flemingate. As Beverley grew in a northerly direction, the older, southern part of the town became the industrial area. Hodgson's great tannery, one of Beverley's historic industries and a major employer, is much reduced in size, but Flemingate, now largely residential, is still a busy thoroughfare in spite of the south-west by-pass. The tiled building (right foreground) 56-58 Flemingate, is reputedly the birthplace of St. John Fisher, though the present construction dates from a period after his death.

The Sun, one of Beverley's oldest inns, dating at least from the 16th century and with fine half-timbering, became the Tap and Spile in September 1994 when it was refurbished in traditional style and took on the name given by its new owners, Beermaster.

Fleming House – for long familiar to Beverlonians as Hodgson's Sports and Social Club, was vacant and in serious decline after the closure of the factory. It is now enjoying a new phase of life as a public house, The Grounds.

The Museum of Army Transport opened in 1983. Financial problems caused its closure in 1997 and some of its exhibits were dispersed. At the time of writing it is again open.

The Museum of Army Transport, converted from Hodgson's building where leather was polished.

Beverley Beck – no longer in commercial use but, with more attention focused on conservation and the removal of pollution, as well as new housing nearby, the waterway is being re-instated as an attractive feature of the town.

The Beck from the fly-over, part of the south-east by-pass opened 1973.

The River Hull – the former shipyard at Grovehill where deep-sea trawlers were built, an industry destroyed by the growing size of trawlers for which the site was inadequate and by the Cod War with Iceland. Vessels had a dramatic side launch. The last trawler built in Beverley was the C. S. Forester, 1969.

The Cemetery, Queensgate.

Allotments, Queensgate. In spite of an incessant demand for land for housing, these allotments survive, with television programmes making gardening more popular then ever.

Looking from Cartwright Lane (foreground) towards Keldgate, with Admiral Walker Road (left) and Queensgate (right): a busy junction unpopular with drivers.

The Leases – the houses built 1934/5 along the line of the old town ditch.

Wards of the old Westwood Hospital due to be replaced by houses. In 1939 the former Workhouse was converted into Beverley Base Hospital, run by the ERCC until taken over by the National Health Service in 1948 and new buildings added. In spite of protests, the decision was taken in 1989 to transfer services to Castle Hill, Cottingham, and to create a community hospital in Beverley.

The new Community Hospital. One resulting problem was that sons of Freemen would now be born in a maternity ward outside the town boundaries (unless born at home), so eliminating their hereditary right to become freemen at the age of 21 and eventually destroying the freemen system. To overcome this problem there is a move to amend the rules by new legislation.

The village of Molescroft has grown enormously in the post-war period and has become a very popular residential area. However, it retains its sense of community and has its own parish council.

The Hayride, a new public house with a name recalling a rural past on the north-east by-pass from Swinemoor to the Driffield road, and a facility for a major new residential area.

Grovehill Bridge over the River Hull, which in 1953 replaced the ferry, then in use again after the earlier swing bridge sank in 1949. The Council commissioned Cook, Welton and Gemmell, shipbuilders) to build the new bridge.

River Hull from Grovehill Bridge – now a waterway for leisure craft.

Weel Tip (officially Household Waste Disposal Site and Recycling Centre) – not a tourist attraction but one of Beverley's most important amenities in an age of throw-away and built-in obsolescence. Since 1964 the tip has occupied much of Hoggard Home Farm.

Automotive Recycling in Anderton's old mill near Grovehill Bridge.

The demolition of a landmark, Paul's (animal feedstuff) Mill, Beckside, earlier Barker and Lee Smith's seed-crushing mill.

Victoria Road – petrol prices at a service station: a record for future historians. In 1985/6 a new road replaced a winding section of Queensgate-Victoria Road and a junction was made for an intended relief road to Hull Road.

Beverley Beck from the Lock.

A reminder of a less mechanical age: the trough, Beckside, intended for horses pulling wagons and barges.

51

SHOPS

Few things reflect social change as immediately as shops, and Beverley has for centuries been the shopping centre for people from a wide surrounding area. The decline of the small family business and the growth of supermarkets and self-service have already been noted. Home-made goods are out-numbered by the ready-made, just as pre-packing involves far less use of the scales on the counter – but far more refuse for the bins. But, even if it is more impersonal, the picture has its brighter aspects. Supermarkets offer an amazing choice of eatables from all over the world, with plenty of opportunities for new gastronomic experiences, hygiene is better, and clothes shops provide a range of colour and style not available to those Beverlonians whose dark outfits feature in so many old photographs.

Carol Bird Interiors, 47 North Bar Within, selling fabrics for furnishing, owned by Carol and John Bird and their son, David. John, a member of the Chamber of Trade, now a town councillor, is Chairman of the committee organising the Festival of Christmas.

Jim Bell's sports shop, 28 North Bar Within, occupies part of the former King's Arms, which later became Scruton's greengrocery and post office.

Their premises occupy part of the Tiger, a Georgian coaching inn with cellars where vast quantities of drink were stored.

Tony Wharton has the shop, Streamers, selling candles and gifts, 43 North Bar Within (the former Tiger Inn) and lives in an upper section known as the Old Coaching House.

Murray Todd, 23 North Bar Within, gentlemen's outfitter, specialising in fashionable clothes, previously worked for the county tailor, John Brown of Saturday Market, for many years before opening his own business in 1968 in adjacent premises (now Robert Gail), moving to this new shop in 1973.

Murray Todd in shop.

Carmichael, Jewellers, 15-17 North Bar Within. John Carmichael, the proprietor, is a member of a well-known local family which owned one of the most celebrated businesses in Hull, and is a cousin of Ian Carmichael, the actor. Francis Johnson, the eminent architect, designed the shop front seen above and the house at the rear.

Mr. and Mrs. Jack Holmes at their shop, North Bar Newsagency, 1 North Bar Within.

Robert Smith outside his shop, Robert Gail.

Robert Gail, china and glass, 21 North Bar Within. Proprietors: Robert and Susan Gail Smith.

North Bar Fabrics, 9 St. Mary's Court, a shopping mall created from Gordon Armstrong's garage – proprietor, Mr. K. Steel.

The Garden Shed, 31 Saturday Market; proprietors: Mrs. Margaret Chastney and Mrs. Rebecca Greenwood, whose plants and flowers are delivered weekly from Holland by North Sea Ferries

– and by the Eradus Dutch flower van.

Flower van – interior.

John W. Adams Ltd., 2-4 Lairgate, at these premises since 1966; the shop enlarged 1981. Proprietors Patrick and Patricia Maské have now been joined by their son, Michael. Managed by Mrs. Andrea Kennedy.

Burgess and Son, 32 North Bar Within – the perfect destination for an outing. Founded by Mark Burgess 1920, taken over by his son Ian and now under Mark's grandson, John. It began as a grocery shop, but the sales of home-made icecream increased until they gradually took over the business.

Haller of Beverley, 2 North Bar Within. Stephen Haller, proprietor, is the grandson of the founder of the firm, which moved from Hull to Beverley in 1979.

Above left and left – Pisces Restaurant and Take-Away, 38 Lairgate. Opened 1990 by Mike Collinson who took over and enlarged a well-known fish and chip shop.

Bridge's Coffee House, 10° Lairgate – proprietors Mr. and Mrs. Peter Ranson.

The Toy Gallery, 64 Lairgate, specialising in traditional toys. Opened by Mrs. J. Kendrew 1990.

The Lairgate Galleries, 10 Lairgate: proprietor David Elwell is a member of a famous artistic family. The business was started by Julia Short, who opened the Norwood Gallery 1978, and had a gallery at Bar House 1983-6.

Andrews and Rogers, 68 Saturday Market, Optometrists.

David Kilford outside his premises, Noel White and Bellamy, gentlemen's outfitters, 11 Landress Lane. Partners Noel White and Peter Bellamy opened their first shop in Hull in the 1930s, later expanding into Hessle and Market Weighton. In the late 1940s Peter Bellamy, now a sole trader, opened a shop in Toll Gavel. David Kilford, who has been with the firm 41 years and is now the proprietor, moved to Landress Lane in April 1990.

Buttons 'n' Bows, 6-7 Saturday Market. The business of Irene Bloom, 34 Saturday Market, was purchased from Irene Hammett (née Bloom) in 1970 by Mr. and Mrs. T. Loft and known at first as Irene Bloom's Button 'n' Bows. Later the business moved to bigger premises at 6-7 Saturday Market and has developed as a haberdashery and stitchcraft shop under Alison Thompson (née Loft).

Prescott Jewellers, 2 Saturday Market, a long-established jeweller's, founded in the late 19th century as a jeweller's and optician's, and now owned by Stephen B. Tomlinson.

The Dolls House, 13 Saturday Market – a new shop; proprietor Mrs. J. Barrett.

Selles, 20 Saturday Market, one of two pharmacies in the town founded by Mr. N. Iddon and now part of a regional chain of similar shops.

Michael Philips started his shop in 1968 selling jewellery, glass and china, and has since been joined by son Philip and daughter Karen. Here Michael holds the trophy which the firm has presented for award each year to the winner of the Kiplingcotes Derby, the oldest horse race in the country.

La Patisserie, 15 Swaby's Yard – bread, cakes, pastry and sandwiches – now the most popular quick lunch for busy people.

North Bar Reproductions, 54 Saturday Market – retains its name from the earlier period when it occupied the former premises of Hasslewood Taylor, North Bar Within. Proprietor: Alan Blondell, who retired in 1999.

H. Fletcher & Sons Ltd., 44 Saturday Market – bread, bakery, greengrocery and delicatessen. A family business established in Hull at the turn of the 19th-20th centuries and opened in Beverley about 21 years ago in premises vacated by Green's after a fire. Now run by David Fletcher.

Market Cross News, 21-22 Saturday Market, sells newpapers, magazines, cards and stationery. Proprietor: Nigel Holmes.

Beverley Camera Centre, 17 Swaby's Yard. Phil Stebbens' shop specialises in all aspects of photographic equipment and supplies.

Sellitt & Soon, Ladygate, occupies the old Beverley Baths – selling furniture and other household items – particularly handy since the town no longer has auction rooms.

Pickwicks, 28 Saturday Market (proprietors: Geoff and Anne Burroughs), specialising in Denby china and stoneware, occupying one of the oldest shops, previously run for many years by Vera Holtby, who sold animal food.

Beverley Building Society, 57 Saturday Market – founded 1866. Its first chairman was James Elwell. Moved from Lairgate 1987.

Viyella, 55-6 Saturday Market,
ladies' fashions, now occupies
another old property, probably
dating from the 16th century. In
great need of restoration, it was
refurbished in 1998.

Beverley Arts and
Crafts Centre, 3
Dyer Lane;
proprietors Mr. and
Mrs. Alan Bailey.

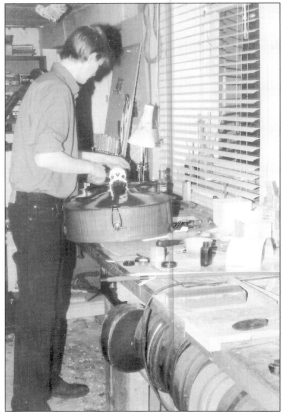

Beverley Music Centre, 14 Norwood (top right)
– For many years a sweet shop patronised by
generations of pupils from Beverley High
School and St. Mary's Junior School, founded
by Mr. G. Pickering around 40 years ago to sell
instruments and sheet music and with a
workshop (bottom right)
where violins and cellos are made.
Now run by Mr. Pickering's daughter,
Rosalind Tunnicliffe with
her husband.

H. E. Akrill Ltd. 18 Saturday Market, gunsmith and sporting equipment. The firm founded in 1828 and now run by Roger Akrill, great-great-grandson of the founder, is the oldest of the family businesses still operating in the town.

Beverley Bookshop, 16 Butcher Row – a well-stocked bookshop operated by brothers Adrian and Martin Gobbi, who attract nationally famous authors to launch new books. The neat Georgian building occupied by their premises may have been built by William Middleton, who was responsible for much fine architecture in Beverley. In the late Victorian period it appears to have been the home of Alfred Crosskill, son of William, the great agricultural engineer.

Briggs and Powell, 59 Saturday Market – one of the few surviving family businesses still going strong at the Millennium as the mecca where household goods, repair items and miscellanea not available elsewhere can be bought. Now run by Susan Cattle.

Races on the Westwood began in 1690 and remain as popular as ever.

Beverley Races 12 August 1998.

Ladies Day, 12 August 1998.

The jockeys' new weighing room, opened 9 May 1998.

Beverley Dancewear and Theatrical Centre, 5 Hengate – Mrs. Jean Elwell provides a unique service in Beverley, supplying dance and ballet shoes.

Charity shop, 12 Dyer Lane, one of a number of charity shops now in the town centre. This one raises funds for Dove House Hospice.

Ideas, 17 Ladygate, a gift shop – proprietors: John and Anne Kerr.

N. Healey, 6 Norwood, a family firm of butcher's, founded 1937 by Norman Healey, father of present proprietor, Adrian Healey (below), in premises previously belonging to Frank Collinson, second son of Francis Collinson of the White Horse. When he began business c1912 it consisted of two cottages.

*The Beverley Bookshop,
with its excellent range of
books, occupies 16
Butcher Row.
Proprietors: brothers
Adrian and (right) Martin
Gobbi.*

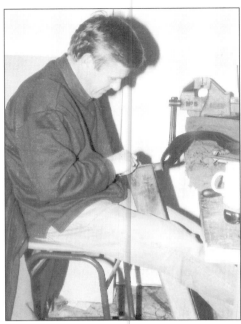

*Patrick Wilkinson, 108 Walkergate – the only
remaining saddler's shop in a horsey town.
At work is Andrew Marchant.*

Peter Robinson.

Beverley DIY and Electrical, 2 Butcher Row. Six years ago, proprietor Keith Norris extended his business to include Beverley Cycling and Walking, a flourishing development managed by his son, Craig, who is keenly interested in such activities.

New, old – and now gone.

Harmony, 28 Butcher Row, stencil designs.

J. C. Peck & Sons, 26 Butcher Row. Stephen Peck is the fourth generation of the family to run the fish and chip shop of high reputation, founded by his great-grandparents in 1915.

Another old business, Harold Robinson, 24 Butcher Row, which closed in 1999. The end of an era came with the retirement of Peter Robinson and the closure of the last butcher's shop in Butcher Row, a business founded by his father, Harold in 1945.

Good 'n' Fresh,
19 Butcher Row.
Previously in Saturday
Market, moved to this
address 10 years ago.
Proprietor: John Dibb.

Arco Intersport, 6 Butcher Row.
Arco, Hull-based firm originally of modest size and
known by its full name, the Asbestos and Rubber
Company, has expanded phenomenally in the post-
war period, specialising in personal protective
equipment and insulation as well as in sports wear
and equipment, as sold in the Beverley shop.

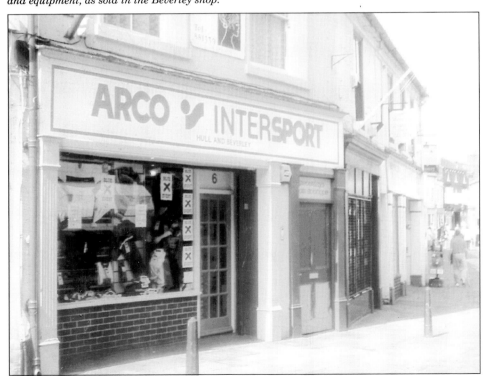

The Orange Tree, jewellers,
10 Butcher Row – a new addition to the town.

Toymaster Beverley, 2 Wednesday Market. Proprietors Richard and Janet Kemp whose business occupies premises where Richard's father established a sweets and tobacco shop in 1951. Richard is keenly interested in Beverley's history and is a former Secretary of the Beverley and District Civic Society and currently Treasurer of the Friends of Beverley Minster.

Safeway Stores, 25 Butcher Row. A supermarket was first opened on this site after the demolition of the Marble Arch Cinema in 1967. Such supermarkets have had a major impact on shopping in Beverley.

Sugar Craft Shop, 36 Highgate – a relatively new business and a valuable acquisition to Beverley as the only specialist shop for cake makers and decorators. Proprietor: Beryl Winn.

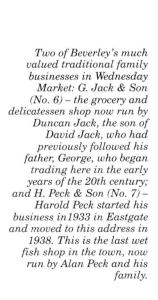

Two of Beverley's much valued traditional family businesses in Wednesday Market: G. Jack & Son (No. 6) – the grocery and delicatessen shop now run by Duncan Jack, the son of David Jack, who had previously followed his father, George, who began trading here in the early years of the 20th century; and H. Peck & Son (No. 7) – Harold Peck started his business in 1933 in Eastgate and moved to this address in 1938. This is the last wet fish shop in the town, now run by Alan Peck and his family.

Molescroft Nurseries, 114 Woodhall Way, a garden centre operated by Roger Wood and his family.

An important piece of Beverley's history, the surviving corner shop and post office, K. Wright's, 2 Westwood Road, at the junction with St. Mary's Terrace – a reminder of the time when the town had a large number of small shops which provided a vital service and acted as a focal point for people of the neighbourhood. Robin Loft is now the proprietor – here serving Dick Gray.

Dales Garden Centre, Long Lane: proprietor Chris Dale – a significant business development in recent years has been the growth of garden centres catering for a leisure activity which has always been popular but has been greatly stimulated by television programmes.

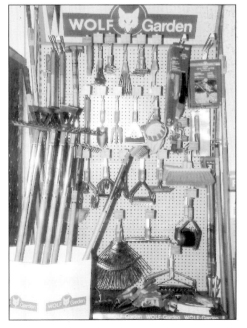

Whittaker's shoe repairs, Mill Lane, founded by Lawrence, father of David (left), who started in the business when he left school in 1959, helped by his nephew, David, (right) since 1983. The dog is Benji, aged 16.

Mill Lane General Stores and Bakery: proprietor Arthur Douglas.

Bridges Coffee House, 10° Lairgate. Proprietors Mr. and Mrs. Peter Ranson.

FESTIVAL OF CHRISTMAS

13 December 1998

Now firmly established as an annual event, the 1998 Festival was estimated to have attracted around 30,000 people to the town.

In a rapidly changing world people tend to look nostalgically to the past. Ted Davy was given the revived post of Town Crier, and is here (bottom left) accompanied by Chris Morris of Driffield, the Pieman.

More olde-worlde street entertainment as part of the Christmas Festival: a juggler outside the Angel, Butcher Row.

Fairs are no longer allowed to take over Saturday Market so a small roundabout such as this was a welcome sight.

73

Christmas biscuits.

Beverley Garland Dancers have kept folk dancing alive.

Changes in local government resulted in the end of Beverley Borough Council and put in doubt the future of the mayoralty. To ensure continuity, while the question of forming a Beverley Town Council was unresolved, Charity trustees were appointed, one of whom was to serve as Mayor. In 1998/9 Councillor Laurie Cross was Mayor, here with Councillor David Ireland, Chairman of East Riding of Yorkshire Council.

'Angels' preparing for the Nativity play at Toll Gavel, Christmas 1998.

The fragrance stall in Saturday Market.

Bill Rice, a former policeman and a popular figure in the town, always identifiable because of his size – and his moustache.

Above right – An Austin 7 displayed in North Bar Within by the Yorkshire Thoroughbred Car Club.

Toll Gavel – a rare sight, full of shoppers on a Sunday.

The Popcorn and Candyfloss stall in Wednesday Market.

Butcher Row – also unusually busy on a Sunday.

The 'teacup' roundabout in Wednesday Market.

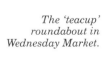

The Mountain Dog – on this occasion helping charity, not lost travellers.

Festival of Christmas,
13 December 1998.

Above left – The festival is now an extremely popular event in the town's social calendar. A stall in Saturday Market.

Left – Kingston Scottish Pipe Band.

Above right – The fairground organ belonging to David Byass of Little Weighton.

Right – A Dickensian touch – roast chestnuts.

Election of the Pasture Masters,
1 March 1999. Under the Pasture Act
1836 the management of the Pastures
is vested in a body of 12 Pasture
Masters elected annually from the
freemen. The presiding officer, the
Mayor of Beverley, may close the poll
if 20 minutes have elapsed during
which no vote is tendered.

The first Town Mayor elected
on 10 May 1999 was
Coun. Mrs. Kate Gray.
(*Courtesy* Hull Daily Mail).

Below right – Beverley
Charter Trustees, who
maintained continuity
between the demise of
Beverley Borough Council
(1996) and the
establishment of Beverley
Town Council: at their last
meeting on 11 February
1999 at County Hall.

After much debate a new
Beverley Town Council was
elected 6 May 1999.
(*Courtesy* Hull Daily Mail).

THE PASTURES

Many towns and villages have their commons: Hampstead has its Heath and Harrogate its Stray. Beverley people, however, consider that their open pastures are unsurpassed and that the preservation of these great green areas has helped to retain the town's distinctive character and attractiveness. 'Pastures' is plural and includes Figham and Swinemoor, but it is the Westwood which arouses the greatest affection and the happiest memories. Its history is long and complicated and at times lawyers have been called in to unravel the technicalities of its ownership. Few, though, would argue that, without its unique system of management by Pasture Masters elected by the Freemen, it would have survived so well as a link with a past when town and country were two inseparable strands in the life of Beverley.

St. Mary's Church from the Hurn – a reminder of Beverley's beginning as a settlement in a low area where beaver lived in the marshy terrain encircled by woods.

The men appointed by the Pasture Masters to look after the pastures are known by their traditional name of neatherds ('neat' is an Old English word for cattle): Jim Cornforth (Westwood) and Mike Botham (Swinemoor).

Return of the cattle, 19 April 1999. One perk of freemen is the right to graze their cattle on the Westwood, though the increasing urbanisation of Beverley means that there is space for non-freemen to rent 'gates' [i.e grazing rights].

Horses on Swinemoor, another of the town's great pastures.

Riding on Westwood – as popular as ever.

Westwood – the Model Aeroplane Club. The Westwood has been a great asset to Beverley, not only by providing wood, chalk, clay (for brick-making) and bark (for tanning) but also offering a most convenient and spacious area for recreational purposes both old and new.

Newbegin Pits where chalk was extracted, later providing a natural amphitheatre for such activities as bull-baiting. The ring to which the poor bull was fettered survives.

Westwood – flying kites.

Beverley High School's 90th anniversary, 26 September 1998. June Atkinson (former pupil and member of staff); Gemma Storey (Head Girl); Irene Bartlett (former pupil and member of staff; Jill Driscoll née Maidment (former pupil).
(Courtesy Hull Daily Mail).

SCHOOLS

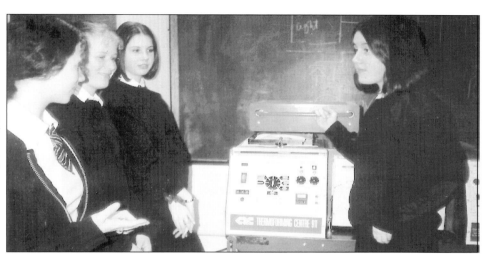

Beverley High School – a symbol of changing attitudes. Girls of Year 11 in the technology construction area.

Beverley Grammar School – a new block under construction.

Beverley Grammar School – pupils of Year 7.

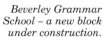

Beverley Grammar School – Year 7 art class.

*St. John's Roman Catholic Primary School,
Wilberforce Crescent – moved here in 1962
from the building in North Bar Without
which had originally been a church and was
to become the parish hall.*

*Swinemoor Junior School. Nine
Rotarians help with weekly reading
classes for 27 children. Here Rotarians
Mac Fleming (l), Jim Richardson (c)
and David Cummings (r) at work.*

*Swinemoor Junior School. Mayor Coun. Laurie Cross distributed oranges on 30 March
1999: the continuation of a custom inaugurated by Alderman William Spencer, headmaster
of Spencer Council School, who left £100 for such an annual distribution. The first was in
1911, and, after the school closed in 1967, the ceremony passed to Swinemoor Junior School.*

Manor Road Nursery School In the new building opened after the demolition of the previous premises as part of the redevelopment of the St. Mary's Manor site.
Head Teacher, Mrs. Y. Norvock with boys' construction set.

Walkergate Infants School.

St. Mary's Church of England Primary School, Eden Road – Year 3 pupils learning about the Ancient Greeks. The building was first used in 1972.

St. John's Roman Catholic Primary School.

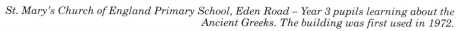

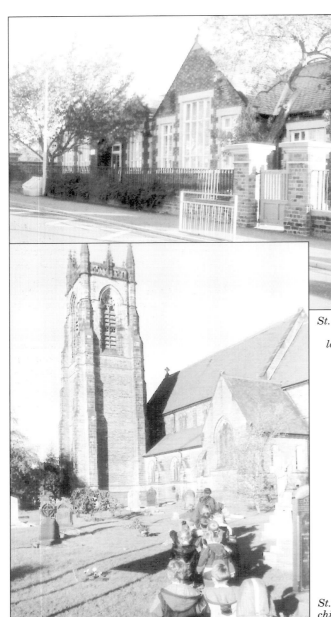

St. Nicholas Primary School – the building of 1915, designed by local architect, Thompson Foley, is still in use.

Technology makes its impact. Year 4 pupils work with computers.

But portakabins now provide additional temporary classrooms.

St. Nicholas Primary School – children on their way to St. Nicholas Church for the Harvest Festival, October 1998.

INDUSTRY

Beverley's industries have had a rough ride over the last 30 years and the impact on employment has been severe. Tanning, once a great industry in the town, has declined to a fraction of its former size, and the hundreds who once worked at Armstrong's no longer crowd the trains from Hull. Shipbuilding, too, another traditional industry, was dealt a mortal blow by the Cod War with Iceland and the consequent decline of fishing from Hull. Even the future of the cattle market, once so crucial to a country town, has looked gloomy. All these losses have been serious matters for the town's economy, and it would be foolish to pretend that 'looking on the bright side' lightens the difficulties. The following pages do, however, show that necessity is the mother of invention. New industries have been developed by the able and imaginative to fill the gaps. Industrial parks where people pursue a variety of occupations in small units have replaced the great companies of the past, and computers and new technology are transforming methods of production and administration. No doubt Beverlonians of a century hence will smile indulgently at what may seem so simple and obvious. All we can say is: at the time it seems very new and rather strange.

Barry Sage, Managing Director of BA Print (founded May 1978 by the late David Cuthbert as BA Press – publishers of the original Beverley Advertiser*), the printers of this book.*

Kwik-Fit, Norwood – the Beverley branch of a national company made famous by its catchy TV jingle about 'a Kwik-Fit fitter'.

Time and Motion, Beckside, founded by Bertram Best 1985; after 18 months taken over by Peter Lancaster.

Hodgson Chemicals Ltd., Flemingate. The firm makes polymers and is the last remaining tannery in Beverley. Tanning was once a major industry in Beverley. William Hodgson established a tannery in 1812, and the firm, taken over by Barrow, Hepburn and Gale in 1920, substantially closed in 1978.

Another traditional Beverley industry – extracting chalk. This spectacular chalkpit on the Westwood belongs to E.C.C. Calcium Carbonates, whiting manufacturers.

The large cone is a dryer.

*A new light industry –
Puzzling People, Old Beck
Road. Justin Thomas cutting
out wooden puzzles.*

*Large permanently-sited
models.*

*As traditional Beverley
industries declined, new
ones developed, one of them
caravan production. ABI
(UK) Ltd., Swinemoor Lane,
was founded 1972 following
the merger of two firms, Ace
and Belmont. Dr. Mike
Isaac, Managing Director
and Gari Klesch, Chairman
(top left).*

Small touring caravans.

*Pyramid Building Systems,
Annie Reed Road –
Brian Fitzgerald applies
adhesive to a base unit.*

*Pyramid
Building
Systems,
Annie Reed
Road.*

*Hodgson
Sealants Ltd.,
Belprin Road –
putting putty
into containers.*

B. & A. Fastening Systems Ltd., Waterside Road, manufacturers of stapling equipment. *Warehouse (above).* *And factory exterior (below).*

John Chapleo, now retired, a former self-employed blacksmith of Norwood Grove: a link with Beverley's earlier industrial history.

Cottingham Joinery, Beckside North, manufacturers of fitted furniture.

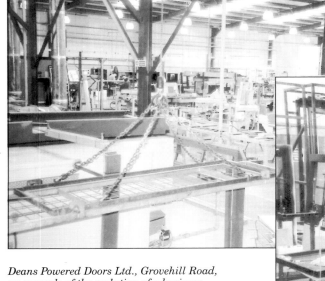

Deans Powered Doors Ltd., Grovehill Road, an example of the evolution of a business. Begun as a family engineering firm in Hull in 1905, it moved to Beverley in 1925, at first manufacturing musical instruments but in the 1930s branched out into public transport fittings.

Sonar Research and Development Ltd., Grovehill Industrial Estate – CAD (Computer Aided Design) model of a shipwreck showing its position on the seabed.
(Sonar Research and Development Ltd.)

Hodgson Chemicals Ltd. – examples of leather produced – once a major industry in Beverley.

John Whitelam of Easi-fit, Grovehill Road, making a fitted kitchen.

ABI (UK) Ltd., Swinemoor Lane – a modern Beverley manufacture, the interior of a large static caravan.

St. Nicholas Primary School, Holme Church Lane: Infants in the Listening Centre.

Swinemoor Junior School, Orange Day, 30 March 1999 – the fruit presented by the Mayor, Coun. Laurie Cross.

Below left – St. Mary's Church of England Primary School, Eden Road – activity session.

Below right – Manor Road Nursery School – PC Bob Sexton, known to the children as 'PC Bob' teaching road drill, and described as just like Dixon of Dock Green – though with a Glaswegian accent.

KTP Ltd., Barcoding, Waltham House, Riverside Road, Kingston Town Photocodes, on the old shipyard site, founded by Bertram Best in 1977 as one of the first barcoding businesses in the country. Chairman: Harry Clarke.

John Carroll replacing a roller for printing labels.

Birchwood Garage, Barmston Road – car maintenance.

Repairing a scanner.

LOCAL GOVERNMENT

Eric Bielby (Mayor 1956-7, 1972-3) and Harry Flynn (Mayor 1957-8, 1969-70), the last two surviving Mayors of the old Beverley Borough Council before its abolition in 1974. The late Albert Meadley was the last Mayor, 1973-4.

Beverley's involvement in local government stretches back over many centuries. Queen Elizabeth I's Charter of 1573 established its Corporation; it was the county town where the East Riding J.P.s met to conduct their business and sit as magistrates; and both Guildhall and County Hall are proud visual symbols of the town's historic role as a seat of government. But no one in those earlier days could have foreseen how local councils would eventually take over responsibility for so many aspects of life. After long years of stability, recent times have seen fundamental, rapid and often confusing changes at both County and Borough level. A new East Riding of Yorkshire Council came into being in 1996 and a new Beverley Town Council was elected in 1999: perhaps auguries of a much needed period of peaceful progress.

County Hall, Cross Street, began life as the headquarters of the East Riding County Council, later occupied by Humberside County Council, and now the East Riding of Yorkshire Council. It also appears in Winifred Holtby's novel South Riding, as the headquarters of the fictional South Riding County Council.

County Hall buildings in Champney Road.

Beverley Guildhall, built 1762, for Beverley Corporation by local architect-builder William Middleton. Local government changes in 1974 brought surrounding villages within the boundaries of a revised borough council, with too many members for the accommodation available in the Court Room, and meetings were, therefore, held in the Council Chamber of County Hall. Further local government changes in 1996 made the Guildhall the property of the new East Riding of Yorkshire Council.

The well-attended public meeting in the Memorial Hall, 27 October 1998, to express concern about Tesco's application to build a superstore on the site of the cattle market. (*Courtesy* Hull Daily Mail).

Top right – The public protest outside County Hall, 15 December 1998, where the application was considered and rejected. (*Courtesy* Hull Daily Mail).

A County Council committee meeting in progress. (*East Riding of Yorkshire Council*).

The disputed land – the Cattle Market site which Tesco wish to use for a superstore.

County Hall – East Riding of Yorkshire Council is a major employer in Beverley. Staff at work in an open-plan office (below).
(East Riding of Yorkshire Council).

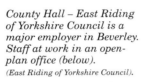

Beverley Cattle Market Christmas stock show, 14 December 1998.

SOCIAL LIFE

Beverley must be the ideal place for people who like 'joining things'. Its range of clubs, societies and sundry organisations is vast and caters for almost every taste and interest: the compilers of this book regret that it is impossible to include every one. Quite a number are connected with churches and provide the opportunity of becoming a member of a community and developing friendships which extend way beyond the regular weekly or monthly meeting. 'Do gooders' tend to be sneered at by those who do nothing, but a lot of unsanctimonious Beverley people derive pleasure from raising large sums for charities in distant places as well as nearer home and – what is often more important – giving practical help. Events like the Early Music Festival, the Chamber Music Festival and the Folk Festival have gained national recognition and create a sense of something exciting happening in the town which even communicates itself to those who never think of buying a ticket.

Walkington Hayride – the re-creation of an idyllic rural past, the Walkington Hayride has become one of the area's great annual events, raising large sums for charity. Organised every year since 1968, this is the hayride on 28 June 1998.

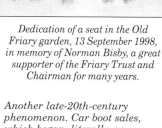

Another lively organisation raising funds for charity, the Beverley Lions held a Police Band concert on 5 July 1998.

Dedication of a seat in the Old Friary garden, 13 September 1998, in memory of Norman Bisby, a great supporter of the Friary Trust and Chairman for many years.

Another late-20th-century phenomenon. Car boot sales, which began, literally, as opportunities for people to dispose of unwanted goods from the boots of their cars, are now a flourishing commercial activity. This one was held at the Racecourse on 30 August 1998.

Old motor cycle rally, Saturday Market, 18 October 1998.

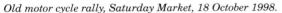

The Inner Wheel's Christmas Fair in aid of charity at St. Mary's Church Hall, 20 November 1998.

Chrysanthemum Show, Memorial Hall, 16 September 1998.

Beverley Early Music Festival, started in 1988, replaces the former Beverley Festival and maintains Beverley's tradition as a town of minstrelsy which dates from the Middle Ages. Robert and Andrea Oliver demonstrate old instruments, 29 May 1999.

The longing for home-baked food in a world of mass production has made the Beverley W.I. Market, held on Friday mornings in the Memorial Hall, a most successful venture. Each member places her name on her own goods and regular customers develop a taste for a particular person's baking.

Beverley Fire Station, opened 1983, one of the best new buildings in Beverley, built in traditional brick, has won architectural awards. It is, however, now manned only by retained (i.e. part-time) fire-fighters. This open day was held 6 August 1998.

Beverley Operatic Society rehearsing their pantomime, Cinderella, *at the Memorial Hall, 7 December 1998.*

The New Year's Day Run 1999 organised by Beverley Lions Club.

A group of Beverlonians near St. Nikolas Church, Lemgo, West Germany, on a visit organised by the Beverley-Lemgo Twinning Association which was established to foster friendship and understanding between the people of the two towns.
(Beverley-Lemgo Twinning Association).

Beverley Minster Music Group whose members sing and play before services.

Beverley Town Detachment, Humberside and South Yorks Army Cadet Force, 22 April 1999, at Norwood Far Grove, where it has been meeting since about 1959. Now commanded by Lt. Jason Britchford.

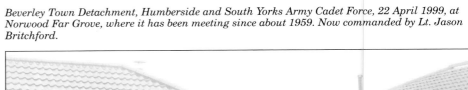

Beverley Brass Band (founded 1969) at practice.

Vista (East Yorkshire Adult Courses) is a flourishing independent organisation arranging courses and visits, both at home and abroad, on the visual arts, architecture, literature, local history and garden design. Professor John Wilton-Ely (lecturer) and Valerie Thornhill (tutor organiser) with members at a meeting held in the St. John Ambulance Hall, 9 March 1999.

Beverley Town Handbell Ringers conducted by John Atkinson, rehearsing in the new St. Nicholas Parish Hall in Holme Church Lane.

Mr. Neil Thwaites making corn dollies on Yorkshire Day, 1 August 1998. Sadly, this very popular figure died in early 1999.

Members of Beverley Theatre Company which (like the Operatic Society) has played an important part in the town's social life for many years, seen here rehearsing for its production of Christmas Carol in the Memorial Hall, 25 January 1999.

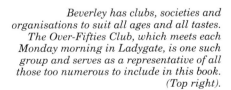

*The Women's Institute
autumn market, 23 October
1998.*

*Beverley has clubs, societies and
organisations to suit all ages and all tastes.
The Over-Fifties Club, which meets each
Monday morning in Ladygate, is one such
group and serves as a representative of all
those too numerous to include in this book.
(Top right).*

*Beverley now has a flourishing Anglo-French
Society and a second 'twin' town, Nogent-sur-Oise,
near Paris, from which a group of children visited
Beverley in April 1999.*

Beverley Fire Station, New Walkergate –
Open Day, 8 August 1998

Beverley Swimming Pool, Mill Lane – 'Mad Hour'
when inflatables are thrown into the water.

Remembrance Day ceremony in the Memorial Gardens,
Hengate, following the service and parade,
Sunday, 8 November 1998.

Beverley Brass Band at practice –
the trombone section.

Meeting of the Holderness Hunt, Boxing Day, 26 December 1998. In spite of current controversy, this is still a very popular event when people come from a wide area to get a breath of fresh air and exercise after Christmas Day's over-indulgence. (Courtesy Hull Daily Mail).

Football, January 1999, near the Black Mill, which lost its sails in 1868.

Golf on the Westwood – Beverley and East Riding Golf Club was formed 1889. The club house is at the old Anti Mill.

Cattle returning to the Westwood, 19 April 1999.

SPORTS

Older residents still talk longingly of the days when Beverley White Star was the football team with a reputation which spread far beyond the town boundaries. Free range facilities on the Westwood have probably helped to establish a tradition of outdoor activities. Riding is as popular as ever it was, and, in a sedentary world, earnest joggers try to look unembarrassed as they stoically use up some of the calories which daily work and routine once consumed. Rugby, soccer, cricket, bowls, squash, tennis (always strong in Beverley), and all the usual sports and games are now supplemented by the current popularity of health and fitness centres and a variety of keep-fit classes where members use all the latest mechanical aids in pursuit of their dreams of a perfect body and eternal youth.

Beverley and East Riding Lawn Tennis Club, established in 1881, hosted 'the tournament of the North' in Victorian times. Its most famous player was Dr. J. Colin Gregory, who won the Australian Open in 1929. Its current membership of 281 includes 134 young players. Coaching is organised for juniors, as shown here at a session, May 1998.

Beverley Bowls Club meeting at the Norwood Park ground.

Beverley Cricket Club playing a match at the Norwood Park ground.

Both codes of Rugby flourish in Beverley

Here Beverley and East Hull Rugby League F.C. play Askham Amateurs at Norwood Park, 16 January 1999.
The club holds the record of being the first amateur rugby league club to beat a professional side.

Beverley Leisure Centre, Flemingate, officially opened 10 September 1990, offers a wide range of sport and keep-fit facilities. Here the treadmill in the 'tone zone'.

And the same day Beverley Rugby Union F.C. play Pontefract at Beaver Park, Norwood

LIFE AT THE END OF THE CENTURY

In an age of self-service and supermarkets, milk is still delivered to the doorstep by electric 'float'.

David Gillyon in action.

Beverley has benefited from being part of the independent Hull telephone system, now known as Kingston Communications. Big changes are afoot at the time of writing with shares offered to the public for the first time and Kingston Communications allowed to supply customers outside its traditional area.

Crash helmets are advisable, even when riding a tricycle.

This has probably been the most difficult section of the book to compile. So many everyday things are taken for granted and accepted as part of the natural landscape that no one can tell which will look quaint and dated in even a few years' time and of far more interest than well documented events. Voting by placing a cross on a piece of paper with a stub of pencil will no doubt be replaced by electronic push-button methods; posted letters may be made obsolete by fax and e-mail; credit cards are already on the way to taking over from money as a means of exchange; and the banning of cars from town and city centres is already mooted. Our selection of pictures can be no more than a random selection of things which Beverlonians of the future may find interesting – or amusing.

Bernard Acklam of Alpha Taxis, 39 Ladygate, whose firm has provided a taxi and bus service for over 40 years. Before starting his own business he drove for Redhead Taxis.

One of the portable polling stations used at the local elections on 6 May 1999.

As traffic increases, 'Lollipop Ladies' – and sometimes gentlemen – provide an essential service escorting schoolchildren across busy roads.

Modern packaging means that many households now produce a large amount of refuse. The local authority made a contract with Biffa to provide this important service from 1 April 1990.

The great expansion of Beverley in recent years has reduced the surrounding green belt. Residents in these new housing developments are sometimes so far from the town centre that 'little buses' have been introduced to provide a regular service.

A family shopping expedition – fathers are no longer embarrassed by pushing prams and push-chairs.

Postman Chris Walker on his daily delivery: one of the most valued personal services which survives in a world of advanced communications technology.

In spite of fax machines and the internet Beverley still manages to fill its post boxes, like this one dating from an earlier reign (top right).

Banking has lost much of its traditional formality, and machines are increasingly used for dispensing cash and statements and providing a variety of other services.

Parking restrictions, and now parking charges, make traffic wardens (with power to impose instant fines) a regular – though not particularly popular – part of the Beverley street scene.

CIVIC SOCIETY

Although this section may appear to contain the only pages devoted to the Beverley and District Civic Society its influence pervades the entire book. Founded in 1961, a time when terrible things were happening to buildings all over the country, and when Mr. C. F. (Bob) Deans and fellow Rotarians became alarmed at the threats to the Beverley they knew, it has been a key factor in making residents aware of the architectural heritage they have inherited and of the need for eternal vigilance in defending it from potential destroyers with facts, figures, logic and professionally presented arguments. The Civic Society has always been at its best and pulled out all the stops when the fight has been hardest. Yet it is the patient, unrelenting attention of its committee members to unexciting and apparently minor matters, month by month and year after year, which has ensured that no planning application escapes without scrutiny and appropriate response. Sow Hill, New Walkergate, housing south of the Minster, St. Mary's Manor, the Regal and now a proposal for a new central supermarket are all major issues for the Society, while placing plaques on interesting buildings and ancient streets has been a quieter way of reminding everyone of Beverley's proud history. But it would be wrong to think that the Civic Society is solely concerned with the past. Its strength is in its continuing role as a guardian of the future.

In its earliest days Beverley was a town surrounded by woods, and Beverley and District Civic Society has been keen to preserve this rural character by planting trees to replace those lost. The Red Oak in Station Square is an example of this policy in action.

The Civic Society has also been keen to have explanatory plaques placed on buildings of note. This plaque on No. 25 Highgate marks the house which Lt. General Oliver de Lancey, who had fought on the losing British side in the American War of Independence, bought on his retirement to Beverley.

From its foundation in 1961, the Civic Society has been involved in debate about major changes to Beverley's townscape. One such issue was the opening up of Sow Hill in 1968 after the demolition of the Globe Inn, along with the creation of a bus station and the building of New Walkergate.

The doorway of the Tudor Guildhall was acquired by antiquarian collector Gillyat Sumner in the 19th century and removed to his garden in King Street, Woodmansey. It was returned to Beverley and re-erected in the grounds of the Old Friary, 28 June 1992.

When Armstrong Patents Ltd. developed its Eastgate site, the 16th-century doorway of the Dominican Friary was saved by being transferred en bloc across the road and installed in the wall of the Old Vicarage, 14 June 1964.

Probably the most controversial new development was the proposal to build houses to the south of the Minster, an issue which went to the highest court in the land, the House of Lords – who allowed the plan to proceed. As a result these houses, Whitehead Close, named in honour of a former headmaster of Minster Boys School, Ald. George Whitehead, were built as part of the scheme for the regeneration of St. Andrews Street.

THE NAME HENGATE PROBABLY DERIVES FROM 'HENN GATA' – THE STREET WHERE HENS WERE KEPT. ANOTHER SUGGESTION IS 'HEN – WEN' A PAGAN GODDESS.

Plaques have been placed near the entrance to old streets recording the derivation of their names and previous names in use.

HENGATE

To mark Walkergate House, the home of William Crosskill, the 19th-century pioneer of agricultural engineering, whose factory was at its peak the most important business in Beverley, a plaque was unveiled by his great-grandson, Ted Crosskill.

BEVERLEY AND DISTRICT CIVIC SOCIETY

WALKERGATE HOUSE

BUILT C 1790 IN A PERIOD WHEN BEVERLEY
WAS BECOMING A FASHIONABLE TOWN OF
ELEGANT HOUSES AND IMPOSING PUBLIC
BUILDINGS. FROM 1866 IT WAS THE HOME
OF WILLIAM CROSSKILL, 'THE FATHER OF
MECHANISED FARMING IN EAST YORKSHIRE'
AND FOUNDER OF THE IRON WORKS IN
MILL LANE WHICH, IN THE 1850'S,
EMPLOYED 800 MEN.

The Civic Society purchased, restored and then re-sold two houses 98/100 Walkergate.

WALKERGATE GREW UP ALONGSIDE A BECK AND WAS
THE STREET OF THE WALKERS WHO SHRANK AND
THICKENED THE NEWLY—MADE BEVERLEY CLOTH.

98-100 WALKERGATE
RESTORED BY THE
BEVERLEY & DISTRICT
CIVIC SOCIETY
1974

The building of New Walkergate was a highly controversial issue which occupied the attention of the Civic Society.